The Secret Origins

Title Page

The Secret Origins Of Judaism

Being an Exposition and Analysis of the Ancient Semitic Cultus from whence Judaism was spawned

By Malik H. Jabbar

Published By

Malik H. Jabbar Publications

P.O. Box 3224

Dayton, Ohio 45401

http://www.NewAgeDatabase.com

COPYRIGHT © 2014 By Malik H. Jabbar

All Rights Reserved. No part of this book may be reproduced or utilized in any form or means, electronic or mechanical, including photocopying, recording, or by any information storage and retrieval systems, without permission in writing from author.

LIBRARY OF CONGRESS CATALOG CARD NUMBER

2014906290

ISBN 10: 1-57154-0113

ISBN 13: 978-1-57154-011-9

The Secret Origins Of Judaism

Table Of Contents

Title Page -- 1

Table Of Contents --- 2

Preface --- 4

Section One: The Judaic Covenant As Embodied In The Seven Jewish Feasts --- 7
    The Perils Of Blind Faith --- 7
    Matters Of Faith --- 9
    The Covenant Examined -- 11
    Religious Evolution Among The Semites ------------------- 16
    Semitic Transition From Paganism To Monotheism ------ 22
    The Passover, Feast Of Unleavened Bread, First Fruits ---- 25
    Linkage of Judaism To Its Primordial Semitic Origins ----- 33
        The Passover Symbolisms -------------------------------- 41
        Feast Of Unleavened Bread Symbolisms -------------- 42
        The Seder Symbolisms ------------------------------------ 49
        Traditional Jewish Seder interpretations --------------- 49
            Items on Seder Menu ------------------------------- 50
            Seder Process --- 50
    Mythological Parallels Of The Passover Festival ---------- 53
    Sacrifices of Lent --- 56
    The Festival Of First Fruits ------------------------------------- 66
    Shavuot, Feast Of Weeks -- 68
        Parallels of the Omer to the Hebrews ----------------- 70
        Parallels of Shavuot and Pentecost -------------------- 72
        Insights into the Traditions of Shavuot --------------- 75
        Notes on Shavuot Traditions ----------------------------- 79

The Secret Origins Of Judaism

Rosh Hashanah -- 82
   Tishri, Month of Lunar-Solar Reconciliation ---------------------------- 87
   Lunar year solar year - Jubilee -- 95
   Yom Kippur --- 98
   Sukkoth --- 113

Section Two: Evolution Of The Sabbath --------------------------- 122
   Babylonian Origin Of The Jewish Sabbath -------------------------------- 129
   Exploring The Menologies Of Sumerian Calendar In Relation To The Jewish Calendar -- 132
   The Sabbath And The 7-Day Week -- 136
   As Regards Hebrew History Verses Hebrew Myth -------------------------- 140
   Death For Violation Of The Sabbath ------------------------------------ 141
   Cultural Traditions Of The Semitic Peoples ---------------------------- 145

Epilogue -- 152

Index --- 155

The Secret Origins Of Judaism

Preface

Monotheism, without doubt, is a irreverent farce and a gross deception. The belief and acceptance of the doctrine of *Divine Revelation* is integral and indispensable to monotheism. **It is upon the shivery foundation of Divine Revelation** that the monotheists propound the alleged legitimacy of their assorted faiths. The wily monotheistic Priesthood asserts unabashedly *the insidious falsity*, that they, of their faiths, have been visited by god in person; and that their religions, namely Judaism, Christianity, and Islam, are bequeathed by god for the salvation of all humankind. They assert further that their *Revealed Books,* that is to say, the Torah, Bible, and Quran convey, by divine sanction, the *Law* and *Guidance* of god for us all. **However**, we, who are rational, do not *for one second* accept the preposterous claim made by the monotheists that god almighty was the author or expounder of either the Torah, the Bible, or the Quran.

This book "*The Secret Origins Of Judaism*" is the first of three books, that I shall offer, *focused on* the lost, hidden, obscured, and occult *origins* of modern religion; from various phases, stretching far back into the ancient past, and from thence onward toward the shenanigans of more recent times. **We shall unveil the astro-theological symbolisms** and other esoteric metaphors extant in modern monotheism; symbolisms that are rooted in the primal and nascent cultures of distant antiquity. **We shall link** our modern religious symbolisms and rituals with their ancient geneses - we will provide clear proofs accompanied by vivid exemplifications firmly reinforced and bulwarked by incontrovertible, rational, and scientific confirmations.

This book, herein, has assuredly accomplished the invalidation of Judaism as a divinely inspired religion. This has been accomplished by *exposing the true non-religious origins* of the Seven Jewish Feasts and other religious rituals innate to Judaism. We have exposed the pagan cores of these rituals and linked them to their primitive origins, to times long ago - long before Judaism became a religion, and before the Hebrews became a tribe. The so-called Covenant between god and the Jews is inextricably

Preface

The Secret Origins Of Judaism

linked with the ritualism embodied in the Seven Jewish Feast, namely *Pesach, Hag Hamatzah, Bikkurim, Shavuot, Rosh Hashanah, Yom Kippur,* and *Sukkoth*. **The Jews claim** that these Seven Feasts were commanded and ordained by god himself as memorials to god's commitment to the Jewish people, and as reminders to the Jews of their specialness in the eyes of god, as well as their obligations to their deity. **This claim** of a covenantal bond between god and the Jews is, of course, a complete and utter fantasy.

The Jewish scriptures, though not divine, are extremely valuable. The scriptures have been held intact for thousands of years, and for that reason alone, are of great intellectual value. Jewish history, as expressed in the bible, is mythological; but be that as it may, the *Jewish Writings* are not mindless myths. **Ancient mythology was the format** by which the Ancients conveyed and preserved precious cultural and scientific data from generation to generation over the centuries and millennia. **The Seven Jewish Feasts** are part and parcel to that ancient encoded wisdom, and as such is the focus of this book. **We have decoded** and unveiled, in striking details, the hidden mysteries of *Jewish ritualism* as expressed in the Feasts, Sabbaths, and other observances of the Jews.

This book *"The Secret Origins Of Judaism"* explores and unveils the *true primitive and secular origins* of the biblical legends and traditions; the Passover, the Feast of Unleavened Bread, the Festival of the First Fruits, Pentateuch, the Jewish Judgment Day, the Day of Atonement, the Feast of Tabernacles. **We have uncovered** the true origins of the strange custom of the Jews wherein for Seven Full Days they are prohibited from consuming *Leaven* - the truth is truly jolting, and has nothing to do with a so-called Exodus from Egypt or wanderings in the Sinai desert. **We have completely decoded** the major symbols of the Jewish Seder rituals. **The true origins of the Sabbath** rituals are unveiled and proved.

The mythological tales of the bible, though non-historical, were not pulled out of thin air. The tales, traditions, and rituals of the bible carry symbolisms of profound ancient truths stretching back into primordial times. The symbolisms, in great part, track cosmic time over the millennia, but also

Preface

The Secret Origins Of Judaism

carry potent cultural, natural, agricultural, scientific, environmental, and philosophical aspects.

Within this book, we trace the *mysterious traditions* and rituals of the Seven Jewish Feasts back to their original *non-religious inceptions*. The true origins of the vaunted Jewish Religious ceremonies are herein explained, including the *underlying non-religious meanings* of the varied Judaic traditions.

The book is divided into two sections, rather than chapters per se, with many Subtopics: **Section One** gives a detailed explanation of the Seven Jewish Feasts; by first explaining the traditional Jewish interpretations of the ceremonies, which is then followed by comprehensive historical analyses and commentaries along with in-depth esoteric insights. Section One is, by far, the longer section. **Section Two** gives a detailed analysis and history of the **true historical origins of the Sabbath,** as opposed to the biblical mythology of god resting on the seventh day, and thus initiating the seven-day week. The structure of Section Two is similar to Section One, and follows the same methodology as utilized in Section One.

Preface

The Secret Origins Of Judaism

Section One: The Judaic Covenant As Embodied In The Seven Jewish Feasts

The Perils Of Blind Faith

What is the true origin of religion? Did god almighty, the alleged creator of all that apparently exist, from out of nothing other than his divine omnipotent will, *actually* write or reveal the Torah, Bible, or the Quran. Is the priestly assertion that god spoke or revealed himself to his chosen prophet Moses through the medium of a Burning Bush rationally understandable or realistically believable? *Exodus 3:1-4 Now Moses kept the flock of Jethro his father in law, the priest of Midian: and he led the flock to the backside of the desert, and came to the mountain of god, even to Horeb. And the angel of the LORD appeared unto him in a flame of fire out of the midst of a bush: and he looked, and, behold, the bush burned with fire, and the bush was not consumed. And Moses said, I will now turn aside, and see this great sight, why the bush is not burnt. And when the LORD saw that he turned aside to see, god called unto him out of the midst of the bush, and said, Moses, Moses. And he said, Here am I.* **Is it reasonable** to accept this biblical assertion as divine truth, or does it ring, to the contrary, with the tone of a fable?

Can we rationally accept that this same Creator god of whom it is said, in the beginning of time, cast the billions of suns (stars) into their several orbits, with their billions of satellites revolving about them or otherwise interacting with them, within untold billions of galactic hierarchies - that this same omnipotent Creator god deigned to take on the human appearance of an itinerant evangelist, in a small Semitic community some two thousand years ago; and that this same individual (Jesus Christ) was the reputed Lord of the Universe incarnate, miraculously conceived and born of a virgin? And further, as we are told by the priesthood, that *god* undertook this human incarnation for the purpose of demonstrating the ultimate human sacrifice - *a sin offering to god* for all of humanity! Is this bizarre expiatory offering of atonement through Jesus Christ, *this literal human sacrifice* as it were,

The Secret Origins Of Judaism

which bears striking parallels in its tone to the pagan sacrificial offerings of varied primitive societies of old - is this tale credible or reasonable?

Is this queer tale of primal human sacrifice, under the banner of modern monotheistic religion, *any different* in its essence to the primitive heathen sacrificial rights of prehistoric eras; wherein, in pursuit of atonement, primal societies (and some relative recent cultures) offered upon raised alters, human sacrifices to their imagined deities? Is our modern religious rite of atonement through the sacrificial slaughter (Crucifixion) of Jesus the Christ *simply a refined version* of the primitive sacrificial rites of our heathen, uncivilized past? Is this replicated tale, along with its parallels to barbaric human sacrifices, intellectually digestible; or does it clearly smack of fable and the delusions of primordial societies who believed that the supernatural forces or deities that controlled nature could be *influenced or bribed by offers of atonement* and blood sacrifice?

Is not the following biblical verse clearly fantastical in its essence? Matthew 1:18-21 Now the birth of Jesus Christ was on this wise: When as his mother Mary was espoused to Joseph, before they came together, she was found with child of the Holy Ghost. Then Joseph her husband, being a just man, and not willing to make her a publick example, was minded to put her away privily. But while he thought on these things, behold, the angel of the Lord appeared unto him in a dream, saying, Joseph, thou son of David, fear not to take unto thee Mary thy wife: for that which is conceived in her is of the Holy Ghost. And she shall bring forth a son, and thou shalt call his name JESUS: for he shall save his people from their sins.

And what would be your response, if told by a Semitic (Arab) merchant of olden times that while he was alone cogitating in a cave, he heard a voice from out of the dark recesses that identified itself as god or his angel, and, in addition, announced that he (the merchant) was the last prophet of god - and yet further, we are told, that this bodiless voice continued to reveal itself to the merchant over the years, culminating in a book labeled as the Last Revelation to mankind from god. How would you judge such an assertion - as truth or folly? *Quran: Sura (Chapter) 32: Verses 2,3: "This is the revelation of*

Section One

The Secret Origins Of Judaism

the Book in which there is no doubt, from the Lord of the Worlds. Or do they say - He has forged it? Nay, it is the Truth from thy Lord, that thou mayest admonish a people to whom no warner has come before thee: in order that they may receive guidance"

Matters Of Faith

In the aforementioned, I have expressed, in a nutshell, the doctrinal claims of *divine authority* made by the monotheists under the three major divisions of *Judaism, Christianity, and Islam.* In my opinion, all three claims to godly sponsorship are patently absurd; but nevertheless, I know that many of my readers will accept *at least one* of these posits as genuine and true - *on the basis of their faith.* In fact faith and/or complete and thorough religious indoctrination are the only possible catalysts that I can think of that would cause any rational or, at a minimum, semi-rational person to accept one or more of these three *irrational* religious postulations as genuine, that is to say, true historical occurrences.

However it must be emphasized that the *fundamental tenet* within all of monotheism, regardless of the denomination, is *belief in Divine Revelation*. In order for you to be a true and genuine monotheist, then you *must believe* and accept without reservation that at least one of the posits offered above is the Absolute Truth. According to the clergy, you must have faith in your religious doctrine *whether you understand it or not*, and if you lack faith you have sinned or fallen short of the mark. **The religionists assert that faith can move mountains**, heal the sick, and that faith marks the path to salvation with god. *Matthew 21:19-22 And when he saw a fig tree in the way, he came to it, and found nothing thereon, but leaves only, and said unto it, Let no fruit grow on thee henceforward for ever. And presently the fig tree withered away. And when the disciples saw it, they marvelled, saying, How soon is the fig tree withered away!* <u>*Jesus answered and said unto them, Verily I say unto you, If ye have faith, and doubt not,*</u> *ye shall not only do this which is done to the fig tree, but also if ye shall say unto this mountain, Be thou removed, and be thou cast into the sea; it shall be done.* <u>*And all things, whatsoever ye shall ask in prayer, believing, ye shall receive.*</u>

Section One

The Secret Origins Of Judaism

Actually, I likewise accept that we can't get through life successfully without faith, that is to say faith in *selected* concepts, people, things, and circumstances. **But I see two types of faith** or *Belief*, particularly distinct in application and rationale, namely *Practical Faith,* and *Religious Faith.* As we maneuver through our daily lives, we are constantly confronted with issues of faith. **We have faith** (belief) that when we are barreling down the road in our cars that when we press the brakes the brake will hold; when we open a can of vegetables we have faith (belief) that the label is true; when we purchase a loaf of bread we have faith (belief) that the product is not contaminated. We have faith (belief) that our dentist is trained to service us efficiently and safely. These matters of *Faith* go on and on as daily issues of life's interactions, and these *descriptions of faith* can be properly described as matters that revolve around <u>Practical Faith or Beliefs</u>, because most of us are *reasonable* and *practical* in how we utilize <u>faith, belief, or trust</u> in the everyday mundane world.

For instance, if we tap on our auto's brakes and the breaks are a bit spongy, immediately we will *reevaluate our faith* or trust in those brakes. If we open up a can labeled corn and find beans therein, we will probably never trust (have faith) in that brand again. If our bread has an unusual taste or odor, we, most certainly, will *reconsider* whether or not the bread should be eaten. And if our dentist injures us, we may lose faith (trust) in that particular dentist, and reconsider allowing that individual to continue servicing our dental needs - **the aforementioned are examples** of the efficacies found in <u>Practical Faith.</u>

However, and to the contrary, <u>Religious Faith</u> operates along guidelines almost diametrically opposite those of *Practical Faith.* As far as I can discern from my observations, for those who are blindly faithful, Religious Faith or Belief is usually *never ever reevaluated* regardless of how many thousands of tests it may seem to fail. The way *religious faith* works, according to my observations, is that the more it fails you then the more you are called to *renew* your faith (trust), <u>not</u> *reevaluate* but *renew* your faith, trust, or belief. If the *faith* or *doctrine of faith* fails you, you are told by the clergy to *reevaluate yourself* and your own actions *but never the faith*

Section One

The Secret Origins Of Judaism

(belief) itself. The clergy tells us that the trials of faith are resultant from the antics of Satan, and that we must not allow Satan to break our faith or *trust in the doctrine* of our faith.

In consequence of this priestly or clerical advice, when we are confronted with religious doctrines and/or circumstances that may, on the face of it, seem blatantly absurd, *we fail to reevaluate* these inconsistencies reasonably and pragmatically. *We have been religiously indoctrinated* so as to *exempt* our religious creeds from logical, rational critiques. So, in compliance with the directions of the clergy, we turn to faith, and then to even more outstanding faith until ultimately we attain the greatest faith of all, which is *Blind Faith*; wherein we believe everything the clergy or scriptures tell us, and question nothing, except perhaps, our own *self worth*, should, per chance, we ever dare to doubt.

Unfortunately, many religious people allow faith to trump and overrule reason - they think that by holding onto the perplexing, puzzling, and confusing tenets of their faiths, *against all odds* they gain points with god. They seem to think that the more they withstand the intellectual or rational torrents of *reason and common sense*, the more worthy they are in the eyes of god because of their unwavering and undaunted faith - their *blind* faith.

The Covenant Examined

But let us move more to the focus of this essay *Unveiling The Secret Origins of Judaism* - our goal is to bring *complete invalidation* to the monotheistic claims of divine patronage. We shall accomplish this goal by rendering a complete expose' on the cherished religious rituals of the so-called *first monotheist* (Hebrews), which rituals, according to their doctrine, were *ordained for them* by god and thereby sanctioned by god himself. Our focus is on monotheism in total, as a fraud and deception, but being that Christianity and Islam are direct descendents of Judaism, we need only to eviscerate the root, that is to say, Judaism; and the branches i.e. Christianity and Islam will wither and decay of their own accord.

Section One

The Secret Origins Of Judaism

We have malice toward none, but neither do we have sympathy. In view of the abject misery and despair caused by the Great Deception of monotheism that has deceived and enslaved the minds of millions under the guise of saving their souls, we must be relentless and unapologetic in our efforts toward disseminating and unveiling truth.

The Jews claim that the <u>seven Great Feasts of Judaism were ordained for them by god</u> Almighty as part of the Covenant between god and they, which (Covenant) commissioned the Jewish nation as god's vicegerent on earth; as a special people, a Priest Nation, as guides and rulers of all humanity. So, *if you believe* that the bible is the word of god, in consequence *you must accept* that all gentiles (people other than Jews) are inferior to the Jews *as decreed by god almighty*, according to the book (Torah) that the Jews say is the direct word of god to them. *Deuteronomy 7:6 For thou art an holy people unto the LORD thy god: the LORD thy god hath chosen thee to be a <u>special people unto himself, above all people that are upon the face of the earth</u>. Exodus 19:5-6 Now therefore, if ye will obey my voice indeed, and keep my covenant, then ye shall be a peculiar treasure unto me above all people: for all the earth is mine: And ye shall be unto me a kingdom of priests, and an holy nation. These are the words which thou shalt speak unto the children of Israel.*

These seven Jewish feasts are the *foundation pillars* on which stand Judaism, and in extension Christianity, and Islam. **If we can successfully topple** these seven religious pillars *by proving their pagan origin*, we will, in effect, have accomplished the *invalidation* of this grand hoax - Judaism, and in consequence Christianity, and Islam also. And this we shall do in sequence, debunking the alleged *divine connections* of the Feasts in succession one at a time.

The seven Jewish Feasts that allegedly form the covenant between god and Israel are as follows:

Pesach (Passover), observed at Nisan 14

Hag Hamatzah (Feast of Unleavened Bread), at Nisan 15 - 21

Bikkurim (First Fruits), observed at Nisan 17

Section One

The Secret Origins Of Judaism

Shavuot (Pentecost), observed at Sivan 6

Rosh Hashanah (New Years), observed at Tishri 1

Yom Kippur (Day of Atonement), observed at Tishri 10

Sukkoth (Tabernacles), observed at Tishri 15 -21

The Jewish <u>Religious Year</u> starts in the Spring proximate to the sun crossing the *Vernal Equinox*. The <u>Civil year</u> starts in the Fall proximate to the sun crossing the *Autumnal Equinox*. **The months of the year commencing in the Spring are as follows:** *Nisan, Iyar, Sivan, Tammuz, Av, Elul, Tishri, Heshvan, Kislev, Tevet, Shevat, Adar*

Now, let us review the bible passages that confirm that the observances of the Seven Jewish Feasts are *central to the covenant* between god and the Jews, that is, according to the claims of Jewish theology. **Please note** that the **bold fonts**, <u>underlines</u> and *comments within brackets* "[ ]" in the following biblical verses are my own, placed for emphasis.

Leviticus 23:1-2 **And the LORD spake** unto Moses, saying, Speak unto the children of Israel, and say unto them, <u>Concerning the feasts of the LORD, which ye shall proclaim to be holy convocations, even these are my feasts.</u>

Leviticus 23:4 **These are the feasts of the LORD**, even holy convocations, which ye shall proclaim in their seasons.

Leviticus 23:5 In the fourteenth day of the first month at even is the LORD'S <u>Passover</u>.

Leviticus 23:6 And on the fifteenth day of the same month is the <u>feast of unleavened bread</u> unto the LORD: seven days ye must eat unleavened bread.

Leviticus 23:9-14 **And the LORD spake** unto Moses, saying, Speak unto the children of Israel, and say unto them, When ye be come into the land which I give unto you, and shall reap the harvest thereof, then ye shall bring a sheaf of the <u>Firstfruits</u> of your harvest unto the priest: And he shall **wave the sheaf before the LORD,** to be accepted for you: on the morrow after the sabbath the priest shall wave it. And ye shall offer that day when ye

Section One

13

The Secret Origins Of Judaism

wave the sheaf an he lamb without blemish of the first year for a **burnt offering unto the LORD**. And the meat offering thereof shall be two tenth deals of fine flour mingled with oil, an offering made by fire unto the LORD for a sweet savour: and the drink offering thereof shall be of wine, the fourth part of an hin. And ye shall eat neither bread, nor parched corn, nor green ears, until the selfsame day that ye have brought **an offering unto your god:** it shall be a statute for ever throughout your generations in all your dwellings.

Leviticus 23:15-16 And ye shall count unto you from the morrow after the sabbath, from the day that ye brought the sheaf of the wave offering; seven sabbaths shall be complete: Even unto the morrow after the seventh sabbath shall ye number fifty days; and ye shall offer a new **meat offering unto the LORD**. [the count of 50 days is synonymous to Pentecost]

Leviticus 23:23-25 **And the LORD spake** unto Moses, saying, Speak unto the children of Israel, saying, In the seventh month, in the first day of the month, shall ye have a sabbath, a memorial of blowing of trumpets, an holy convocation. Ye shall do no servile work therein: but ye shall offer **an offering made by fire unto the LORD.** [the first day of the seventh month is Rosh Hashanah, the Civil New Years]

Leviticus 23:26-28 **And the LORD spake** unto Moses, saying, Also on the tenth day of this seventh month there shall be a day of atonement: it shall be an holy convocation unto you; and ye shall afflict your souls, and offer an offering made by fire unto the LORD. And ye shall do no work in that same day: for it is a day of atonement, to **make an atonement for you before the LORD your god**.

Leviticus 23:34-36 Speak unto the children of Israel, saying, The fifteenth day of this seventh month shall be the feast of tabernacles for **seven days unto the LORD**. On the first day shall be an holy convocation: ye shall do no servile work therein. Seven days ye shall offer an offering made by fire unto the LORD: on the eighth day shall be an holy convocation unto you; and ye shall offer an offering made by fire unto the LORD: it is a solemn assembly; and ye shall do no servile work therein.

Section One

The Secret Origins Of Judaism

Leviticus 23:44 **And Moses declared** unto the children of Israel **the feasts of the LORD.**

So, in the above verses from the twenty-third chapter of Leviticus, as well as in numerous other verses of the bible, we read that the Seven Jewish Feasts are actually major religious events ordained and sanctioned by god almighty. The scriptures tell us that these Feasts are an integral element of the Covenant between god and the Jews or the Children of Israel.

The Hebrews claim that the *Seven Jewish Feasts* have been ordained for them by god himself. This claim, by the Jews, of divine sanction is not a trivial matter; because Judaism itself is structured upon the claim of the Jews to a divine partnership with god. **The observance of the Seven Jewish Feasts are a requisite component** of the so-called covenant between they and god; therefore **if we discover that this claim is fraudulent**, then the whole house of Judaism is brought down in disgrace, and not only Judaism, but all other monotheists who have accepted the priestly lineage of Abraham, Jacob, and Moses as divine mediators between god and mankind.

If we prove that the covenant is bogus, that such an agreement between god and a Semitic tribe never took place, and likewise that the slavery of the Jews (Israelites) in Egypt is not historical, then it follows in consequence that the biblical Moses is not historical. **And if the biblical Moses is not historical**, it behooves us to question the historicity of Jacob and his twelve sons, as well as Isaac and Abraham. **The question needs to be answered** - why can't any of these alleged divine patriarchs be found in any credible historical chronicles! This line of patriarchs only shows up in the bible and Quran; and, of course, the bible and Quran are not chronicles of history, but rather books that *promote* their separate religious doctrines.

Let it be remembered - the seven Jewish feasts form the basis for the so-called covenant between god and the Jews. The covenant was struck, according to the bible, at the time the Israelites were delivered from slavery in Egypt. **Of course our mission** within this book is to invalidate the Jewish claim to divine patronage by exposing the true pre-Judaic pagan origins of the *Seven Jewish feasts*.

Section One

The Secret Origins Of Judaism

Religious Evolution Among The Semites

It must be understood that Judaism and the other major religions as well, were all evolved from *primitive* cultural systems that practiced Nature Worship, and Animism; that is to say the assignment of unseen mystical deities as the driving forces, or we might say compelling spirits, envisioned by those ancients as the manipulators of the natural environment. This animistic attitude prevailed amongst the ancient Semites and various primitive cultures, while in their *prehistoric,* inceptive or embryonic, developmental stages; *before* their religions or dogmas attained their *historical* form and subsequently their *recent and modern forms*. The primary focus of early primordial Man, first emerging into awareness of himself as an *intelligent animal*, was not toward a glorious, outwardly charitable, and benevolent deity as pictured in the Garden of Eden tale. They were in search of a *supernatural benefactor* to aid them in their struggles against the enveloping, oppressive and combative forces (spirits) of nature, which they confronted daily.

The most pressing and primary concern of primordial Man was his *immediate survival* within his earthly habitat. They sought out and importuned their imagined gods through sacrificial and ritualistic rites of atonement and self flagellation. Absent profuse animal hair, Man was naked so he needed clothing; absent his canines and claws, he was defenseless so he needed weapons. He needed shelter to protect himself from the elements and predators, and the tools thereby to fashion those shelters. He needed food that would nourish him, and not sicken or poison him, hence he needed tools and weapons by which to secure his sustenance. All of the above are practical needs, mundane, immediate, and worldly. The relationships of the prehistorical primitive societies to their *imagined deities* were therefore necessarily intertwined with their day to day struggles to combat and withstand the oppressive and repressive forces of nature, their ecological environment.

All of the primitive gods visualized or worshipped by primitive Man *reflected traits of nature*, hence you have Wind or Storm gods, Rain gods,

Section One

The Secret Origins Of Judaism

Earth gods or goddesses, River gods, Sun gods, Moon gods or goddesses, Star gods, Fire gods, Tree gods or goddesses, Vegetation gods, etc etc. All of the primeval deities carried names or descriptions that described the *attributes of the natural environment*, its interactions and reactions; that is to say the Wind, Fire, Earth, and Water, Light, Darkness, Birth, Death, etc because these are the forces most germane to Man's survival.

Over the generations, as humanity evolved intellectually, and became more adept and skilled at combating and harnessing the forces of nature, *their perceptions* of the deities were subsequently *elevated*. They then sought after deities, not only as aids and guides in their daily and seasonal struggles for survival in the unrelenting war against the inimical forces of nature (devil or evil forces = evil spirits); but now, they also, *in keeping with the social demands of their advancing societies*, sought guidance and aid from the deities in matters concerned with the higher values of life; such as family and community structure, ethics, morality, judicial systems and so forth. **But initially**, when in their most primitive stages in those dark distant primordial ages, mankind's focus was locked on day to day survival, and that is why they conjured or summoned gods (created from the wells of their imaginations) *that had immediate relevancy* to their need to withstand the hostile natural forces (evil spirits) within the environment, which (forces) in their primitive perspectives were aimed directly at them.

In their efforts to combat and/or appease those perceived *evil spirits* (i.e. unseen controllers of the forces of nature), primitive Man incorporated offers of wealth (crops, artifacts, weapons, etc) prayers or devotions, self flagellation, and blood sacrifices of animals and people so as to appease and/or please the unseen Nature Gods (those unseen forces/spirits that produce earthquakes, storms, droughts and so forth). **And from this mix was born the systems** of atonement and sacrificial rites to the gods, that still prevail in our cultures down to this very day; veiled under the artificial veneer of religious traditions. It was not until the passing of many centuries as mankind became more adept, skilled, knowledgeable, and functionally aware of the vicissitudes of nature, that they, with improved insight and intellection began to refine their worship of the gods.

Section One

The Secret Origins Of Judaism

As Man became more and more learned and civilized over the centuries and the millennia, he began to adjust the terms by which he labeled his gods, and he also adjusted the descriptions and rituals by which he related to his gods. This transitional phenomena (evolution from primitive religions to modern religions), *accomplished through methods of cultural adaptations*, was worldwide and evolved among societies throughout the whole planet, *including the Semitic cultures* from which the Jews have descended.

Judaism is not a gift from god but rather the result and outgrowth of Semitic culture, and has not been bequeathed to us or the Jews by god. Judaism is a cultural manifestation resultant from the traditions, rituals, and *customs of the Semitic people*, of which the Hebrews, so-called Israelites or Jews are a part.

We intend to prove, as noted earlier within this essay, that the *Jewish religious customs*, which the Jews have claimed were bequeathed to them by god, are, in fact, no less than the workings and constructions of the Jewish sacerdotal classes, the priesthood. **The Jewish religion was invented** by the Jewish priesthood, and in its invention it was *adapted* to the primitive pagan or nature customs and traditions of the ancient Semites of Mesopotamia, Arabia and thereabouts. **Therefore** in order to prove and expose the *true* cultural nativity or origins of Judaism, which clearly and soundly contradicts and invalidates their claims to divine patronage, we will examine each of the seven Jewish feasts, which are the *Pillars of Judaism*. We will define their ritual activities, and then prove that these ritual activities are, in fact, adaptations to ancient Semitic pagan rites.

All primitive people had Special Days or rituals that marked the changing of the seasons, most generally noted when the sun crosses, in turn, the four cardinal points i.e. the vernal equinox, summer solstice, autumnal equinox, and the winter solstice. This was important because of the tremendous impact of the changing seasons on Man's habitat. It was incumbent that Man prepare for the changes in the environment brought on by the changing seasons.

Section One

The Secret Origins Of Judaism

The *signals* for the various preparations *were the positions of the sun* relative to the four cardinal points. Of course, the various *primordial* rituals, traditions, and customs that accompanied the changing of the seasons are the matrix from which our modern religious holidays have spawned - **this is why** all of our major religious holidays are proximate the celestial cardinal points. Also, this, the above noted, is why all of the major Jewish holidays are marked by the cardinal points. Witness Quote from my book *The Astrological Foundation Of The Christ Myth Book Four*: The history of ancient mans emergence from the nomadic state into settled communities with organizational structure, agriculture, animal husbandry, and the partitioning of permanent hereditary duties to families and/or members of the community, the nascent formations of Military, Royal, Ecclesiastical and Artisan Class structures with centralized authority and rules of conduct is Key to pinpointing the embryonic cultural and social traditions that over the millennia would eventually evolve into the social force popularly known today as revealed religion, inclusive of its social creeds and spiritual concepts. In fact all forms of religion practiced in this (our) era can be traced to this same type source or origin. Our religious philosophies are an evolutionary reflection of mans historical interaction with nature, shielded in myth and fable. These myths and fables of the distant past have evolved into our modern religious concepts. There is no truth to the concept of Revealed Religion (Revelation From a god (supernatural spirit) to a messenger (prophet)) – all religious beliefs are the result of mankind's social evolution and the Key to interpreting the myths and symbols embodied therein is found when we accurately separate actual history from mythical history, and then evaluate the actual history dispassionately – and this task is not easily accomplished

Another important point that must be emphasized, as we enter into the analyzation and decipherment of the true meanings and origins of the *Seven Jewish Feasts*, is that there are *two major categories* (and multiple sub-categories) of symbolism or mythology that mirror the ancient rituals and traditions of primordial Man, namely *Environmental* Symbolism or Mythology, and there is *Scientific* Symbolism or Mythology. I use the two terms *Environmental Mythology*, and *Scientific Mythology* so as to differentiate between the two major forms of mythology discussed in my books, the one i.e. the *Environmental*, is rudimental and basic, and the other i.e. the *Scientific*, is reflective of profound erudition.

Section One

The Secret Origins Of Judaism

The earliest prehistorical forms of mythology were *environmentally* motivated at the most basic level of existence whereas the primordial societies surmised that the forces of nature were controlled and manipulated by unseen spirits. Those early primitive aboriginals did not envision that the seemingly fickle forces of nature, in truth, functioned by design; that these forces were naturally cyclical, and inherently tied ecologically to *natural patterns,* activated and sustained in response to the integrated teleological dynamics of nature's immutable laws. Nor did they understand that these immutable Natural Laws caused pleasant and unpleasant climatic conditions (as perceived by the human species) in cyclical procession, devoid of the conscious intent of any entity, mortal or immortal; but rather as ordained and compelled by the limiting and expanding forces innate to nature. They did not understand, as many of us do, that those myriad volatile and hostile forces of nature, that at times, seemed as though targeted right at them, in truth, lacked emotional volition or conscious will. As a side note, I must say that I am truly stunned and bedazzled that in this day and age, the 21st century, that there are millions of people who yet believe that inclement weather or earthly upheavals, and natural disasters are signs and warnings from an angry god because of our sins; or warnings that Judgment Day approaches. This shows that little has changed in the psyches of the hoi polloi over countless millennia. Many among us are just as superstitious, or nearly so, as our benighted primordial ancestors of countless ages gone by.

This lack of knowledge or understanding of the natural environment, among the earthly natives, engendered animism - the belief that unseen spiritual beings, demons, deities, and the like were the initiators of natural phenomena. **Furthermore they imagined** that these unseen spirits not only possessed volition and temperament, but were also emotional and passionate like themselves, and likely to respond to human *entreaties* and *offerings,* such as an earthly king might respond to his subjects pleadings and gifts. The focus therefore of these early mythologies (fabled belief systems) centered about simple, unsophisticated people and their interactions with the mercurial faces (forces) of nature - good spirits and bad spirits, angels and demons, saviors and oppressors - to the wildest or furthest extents of their imaginations and superstitions.

Section One

The Secret Origins Of Judaism

The most cherished goal, hope and aim of these primordial populations can be summed up in one word - *Salvation,* that is to say the certain and permanent release from the cycles of their recurrent torments in the never ending struggle to survive within their earthly habitat. Their concocted mythologies, *as developed in the early primeval stages* of human civilization, were created in reflection of the stresses, hopes, fears, interactions and perceptions of the earthly environment that confined them; mythologies that were shackled by superstitions, and the meager intellectual capacities of the populations of those archaic eras.

Scientific mythology represents another paradigm altogether, a *higher* cognizant plane reflective of and accompanying the intellectual ascendancy of man, apart and above the benightedness inherent in some aspects of environmental mythology. Scientific mythology tracks the elevation of the human race industrially, scientifically, socially, rationally, economically, and spiritually; it accompanies the emergence and development of the enlightened consciousness in the human species.

Under Scientific mythology, when properly decoded, it is evident that Man no longer saw himself as *merely* an intelligent animal, but rather as *ascendant spiritual beings,* temporarily encased or gestating in matter or as expressed in some phases or graduations of the mythology - *at war with matter*; in route to a divine destiny, that is, as regards the metaphysical phase of the symbolism, which we shall cover later in our series.

Scientific Mythology is the rendering of highly advanced societal knowledge in a cryptic mythological format. Scientific mythology reflects the Earth Sciences, Astronomy, Biology, Agriculture, Ethics, Government, and so on. Scientific Mythology is an arcane language of Signs and Symbols that we may find cryptically expressed in religions, oral traditions, art, literature, architecture, customs, holidays, language, numbers, and even games and attire, and so forth.

Of course our main concern or focus, in this essay, is Astrotheology and its assorted implications in our culture and religions. And of immediate concern is the decoding of the curious rituals embodied in the seven Jewish feasts

Section One

The Secret Origins Of Judaism

traditionally practiced by the Jewish populations of the world; rituals alleged as having been decreed by god as integral to a so-called covenant between god and the Jewish people.

Semitic Transition From Paganism To Monotheism

Societies have invariably, since time immemorial evolved from stage to stage; and will forever continue evolving, into infinity, as we march through the aeons of time - from generation to generation, from century to century, and from era to era. **Also**, as is readily understood by most, *evolution requires adaptation* - **but not** just anatomical adaptation or biologically based adaptation, as with the natural evolution of the species in adaptation to its habitat. **Societal evolution itself requires** *cultural adaptations* so as to keep pace with the ever increasing sophistication of some members of the citizenry, **and also**, cultural modifications are required simply to advance or elevate society intellectually as the burgeoning generations unfold. **In addition, there are other factors**, distinctly nefarious and insidious, and artfully associated with the strategies of the political and religious elite that significantly impact the modes of cultural adaptations undergone by various societies - this is significantly true of ancient cultures, and, of course, applicable to the present era.

Cultures, as they evolve, must adapt to the evolving intellect and perceptions of its members. Cultures, as they evolve intellectually, *must change with the times*, changes caused by the improved acumen of the populace that causes them to lose faith and to reject old ways and customs in favor of new modes in keeping with the transient so-called modern ages. I say *transient* modern ages because every age, in its own season, is a *modern age* till supplanted by or merged with its successor. Each generation lives in its own modern age. We, in this 21st century live in the modern age, *but in turn*, so did the inhabitants of the 19th century, the 12th century, the 3rd

Section One

The Secret Origins Of Judaism

century, and on and on as far back as the records or memories of the ages can take us[1].

But by what methods have societies historically evolved their cultures - most certainly, <u>not</u> by totally discarding their ancient customs and traditions into the trash heaps of time. For certain the customs that we now cherish go back, in many cases, for thousands of years; but we have adopted and <u>adapted</u> *modern forms* to our cherished traditions - such are the ways of cultural evolutions. **As societies grow and evolve over time, they change** in many noteworthy but nevertheless superficial ways. **The core of the culture tends to remain unchanged**; it (the core) is overlaid or merged *but not destroyed*. **A perfect example** of this is found above in my references to Jesus Christ as a *modernized version of ancient Human Sacrifices* to pagan deities pursuant to tribal atonement. The sacrificial Jesus, *at the core,* <u>is no different</u> in essence than the sacrificial victims offered up by the pagans of yore to their deities. We have cloaked the *Sacrificial Offering* (Jesus) of our modern age with a new style fitting to the times, but the <u>underlying message</u> of *pagan human sacrifice* in pursuit of redemption or atonement remains intact.

The layering or merging of our modern religious customs upon and into pagan rituals, through a process of <u>adaptation,</u> is palpably evident throughout our cultures: **we have layered** our Christmas Festival upon ancient pagan festivals that celebrated the birth or rebirth of the sun at the Winter Solstice. **We have layered** our Easter festival upon the ancient pagan festivals that celebrated the birth of Spring at the Vernal Equinox. **The Muslims** have designated the Hajj as one the five pillars of Islam, but actually, this rite of pilgrimage to Mecca was practiced by the pagan Arabs untold years before the prophet breathed his first breath - this migration of the Hajj ritual into the incipient Islamic faith clearly reflects the cultural

---

[1] Of course, there have been periods of cultural stagnation whereas societies change little over multiple generations.

Section One

The Secret Origins Of Judaism

evolutionary process of *adaptation*, and not the issuance of a divine decree. **Through the Process** *of Cultural Adaptation* the **core** of the ancient *pagan ritual* is **overlaid with a modern religious veneer, and given a new artificial religious interpretation.** And it follows in suit that the vaunted *Jewish festivals* likewise have been *layered upon an ancient pagan core.* **Our focus going forward** is the *explanation* of how the layering of a mythical religious veneer upon a primeval pagan Semitic core was accomplished.

A pretty good explanation of the *transition process* of paganism to modern religion, although in a more recent time frame than the *primordial eras* on which we are now focused, can be found in my book *The Biggest Lie Ever Told, 4th Edition -* **See Quote:** When Christianity evolved at the dawn of the Pisces era, the problem that faced the intellectual leadership (religious, political, financial alliance) of that time was How to elevate their society to a higher degree. They (the priesthood) could not break the influence and control that primitive nature worship exercised over the masses. So they decided to do the next best thing. They decided to convert (evolve or merge) idolatry into emerging modern Christian religion. They decided to transfer the old pagan customs (modified or renamed) into the new religion. In other words, they conceded to the populace the right to keep their old practices, and rituals, (for the most part) but they labeled the rituals with different names and new applications. They couldn't change the people, in terms of their ingrained customs and habits; so instead, they sought to change the appellations of the popular pagan deities. They changed the names and/or applications of what the people worshipped; and <u>introduced modified reasons for the traditional practices</u>, thereby continued and retained under a new Christian guise

Before we can elucidate a clear and comprehensive explanation of the Judaic adaptation of ancient *pre-Judaic rites and rituals* into the Judaic religion, we must first familiarize ourselves with Judaic rituals and customs. After we have made an explanation of the traditional Jewish customs and their purported significance, the path will be open for unveiling and proving the innate cultural linkage between the *Judaic religion* and the *belief systems and rituals* of the primordial Semites. Let us now patiently review the pertinent Jewish rituals that accompany the Passover season. After the

Section One

The Secret Origins Of Judaism

review is complete, we will unveil and explain the seminal linkage of these Passover rituals to various pre-Judaic traditions of the primordial Semites.

The Passover, Feast Of Unleavened Bread, First Fruits

The Jewish religious year begins in the month of Nisan (Abib), which occurs at the first New Moon proximate the sun passing over the vernal equinox at the dawn of spring. **The first festival** (Feast) of the Jewish ecclesiastical year is **Passover** which begins on the 14th of the month of Nisan. **They select the Passover Lamb on the 10th of the month**, and hold it till the 14th of the month. On the evening of the 14th they slaughter the animal, and at the beginning of the 15th, which commences at 6 PM that evening, they celebrate the Passover. *Exodus 12:3-6 Speak ye unto all the congregation of Israel, saying, In the tenth day of this month they shall take to them every man a lamb, according to the house of their fathers, a lamb for an house: And if the household be too little for the lamb, let him and his neighbour next unto his house take it according to the number of the souls; every man according to his eating shall make your count for the lamb. Your lamb shall be without blemish, a male of the first year: ye shall take it out from the sheep, or from the goats: And ye shall keep it up until the fourteenth day of the same month: and the whole assembly of the congregation of Israel shall kill it in the evening.*

The reason given by the Jews for the celebration of the Passover feast is that this feast, in the month of Nisan (Abib), marks the occasion of their deliverance from bondage in Egypt. *Deuteronomy 16:1 Observe the month of Abib, and keep the passover unto the LORD thy god: for in the month of Abib the LORD thy god brought thee forth out of Egypt by night.*

The bible asserts that the tenth plague of god against Egypt, that is to say, *the plague of death* to the *First Born* of Egypt was the plague that finally convinced Pharaoh to release the Israelite slaves. *Exodus 12:29-32 And it came to pass, that at midnight the LORD smote all the firstborn in the land of Egypt, from the firstborn of Pharaoh that sat on his throne unto the firstborn of the captive that was in the dungeon; and all the firstborn of cattle. And Pharaoh rose up in the night, he, and all his servants, and all the Egyptians; and there was a great cry in Egypt; for there was not a house where there was not one dead. And he*

Section One

The Secret Origins Of Judaism

called for Moses and Aaron by night, and said, Rise up, and get you forth from among my people, both ye and the children of Israel; and go, serve the LORD, as ye have said. Also take your flocks and your herds, as ye have said, and be gone; and bless me also.

However, it is alleged that the First Born of Israel escaped the Plague of Death because they followed the instructions of god to Moses that they smear the blood of slaughtered lambs upon the lintels and doorposts (side posts) of their houses as a sign to god, so that **when god traveled through Egypt on his death mission, he <u>Passed Over</u> the houses smeared in blood**, knowing by reason of the blood splattered upon those houses that therein dwelt Israelites, thereby sparing his chosen from the deaths of *their* (Hebrew) firstborn. *Exodus 12:21-23 Then Moses called for all the elders of Israel, and said unto them, Draw out and take you a lamb according to your families, and kill the passover. And ye shall take a bunch of hyssop, and dip it in the blood that is in the bason, and strike the lintel and the two side posts with the blood that is in the bason; and none of you shall go out at the door of his house until the morning. For the LORD will pass through to smite the Egyptians; and when he seeth the blood upon the lintel, and on the two side posts, the LORD will pass over the door, and will not suffer the destroyer to come in unto your houses to smite you.*

Another curious part of this festival season is the *Feast of Unleavened Bread* which merges with the Passover event - for seven whole days the Jews are prohibited from possessing or eating any item that has touched or contains leaven. *Exodus 12:18 In the first month, on the fourteenth day of the month at even, ye shall eat unleavened bread, until the one and twentieth day of the month at even.*

And also, integrated within *Passover* and the *Feast of Unleavened Bread*, the faithful Jews likewise observe (according to biblical tradition) a ritual known as Bikkurim or *First Fruits*. **First Fruits represent the first fruits of the harvest**, whereas the Jews are <u>instructed by god</u> to do the following: gather some stalks (sheaf) of their crops, take them to the priest (Rabbi) who shall, in turn, wave these stalks about the Temple as an offering to god - sounds rather bizarre to me, but such is the requirement of god almighty according to the bible. *Leviticus 23:10-11 Speak unto the children of Israel, and*

Section One

The Secret Origins Of Judaism

say unto them, When ye be come into the land which I give unto you, and shall reap the harvest thereof, then ye shall bring a sheaf of the firstfruits of your harvest unto the priest: And he shall wave the sheaf before the LORD, to be accepted for you: on the morrow after the sabbath the priest shall wave it. **This activity**, that is the harvest ritual of waving the grain stalks before the Jewish god commences the 50 day count-down to the festival or feast of *Shavuot* on Sivan 6. *Leviticus 23:15-16 And ye shall count unto you from the morrow after the sabbath, from the day that ye brought the sheaf of the wave offering; seven sabbaths shall be complete: Even unto the morrow after the seventh sabbath shall ye number fifty days; and ye shall offer a new meat offering unto the LORD.*

The Jewish harvest festival of Shavuot is synonymous, in its religious context, to the **Pentecost** of the Christians - it was during Shavuot that Moses is alleged to have ascended **Mount Sinai** to have a conversation with god and received the heralded **Ten Commandments**. It was also during Shavuot, The Feast Of Weeks, on Sivan 6, that the divine spirit allegedly descended upon the assembly of the seemingly forlorn disciples of Jesus at the occasion of what we now call Pentecost culminating in the miraculous **Speaking in Tongues.** *Acts 2:1-4 And when the day of Pentecost was fully come, they were all with one accord in one place. And suddenly there came a sound from heaven as of a rushing mighty wind, and it filled all the house where they were sitting. And there appeared unto them cloven tongues like as of fire, and it sat upon each of them. And they were all filled with the Holy Ghost, and began to speak with other tongues, as the Spirit gave them utterance..*
Floating cloven Tongues appearing out of nowhere and somehow attaching themselves to people and speaking! In diverse languages! Filled with the Holy Ghost and controlled by Spirits! This is so weird!

Let me remind you, as we proceed with our delineation of the seven Jewish feasts, that the rationale given to us by the Jews for the continual and perpetual observance of these primitive and baffling feasts is that the feasts are an integral contingent of the bargain (covenant) between they and god. As the story goes, god required from the Jews, as the benefactor and liberator of the Israelites from Egyptian bondage, that the Jews shall forever hold in remembrance god's special favor to them by reason of that liberation; by observing these feasts in perpetuity as *divinely mandated memorials* to their emancipation from Egyptian slavery.   *Exodus 13:8-10*

Section One

The Secret Origins Of Judaism

And thou shalt shew thy son in that day, saying, This is done because of that which the LORD did unto me when I came forth out of Egypt. And it shall be for a sign unto thee upon thine hand, and for a memorial between thine eyes, that the LORD'S law may be in thy mouth: for with a strong hand hath the LORD brought thee out of Egypt. Thou shalt therefore keep this ordinance in his season from year to year.

The biblical traditions of the Passover season, along with the standard rituals now practiced by modern Jews are these: First off, on Nisan 10, they select the animal that shall serve as the Passover. The term *Passover* refers to the sacrificial lamb itself as well as to the *deed* of god passing over the Hebrew houses during god's death march through ancient Egypt whereby he (god) killed all the first born of Egypt but spared the Jewish first born by reason of his special devotion to the Jewish people. The sacrificial lamb, thus obtained on the tenth of the month, must be without spot or blemish, with no imperfections and no broken bones. *Exodus 12:5 Your lamb shall be without blemish, a male of the first year: ye shall take it out from the sheep, or from the goats: Exodus 12:46 In one house shall it be eaten; thou shalt not carry forth ought of the flesh abroad out of the house; neither shall ye break a bone thereof.* **The lamb is sequestered and held captive**, while awaiting its slaughter on the evening of Nisan 14 which marks the start of the official day of Passover at 6 PM on Nisan 15. This (Nisan 15) is the *same evening* as Nisan 14 - being that the Jewish day starts at *six o'clock in the evening*.

The night before the Passover of Nisan 15 marks the ritual of *Bedikat Hametz*. Bedikat Hametz is an extremely rigorous, some might say fanatical, search of the entire premises, house, out buildings, and lands for any remnant of leaven (Hametz). The tiniest bit of leaven must not be allowed to remain on the premises when Passover arrives *the next evening* - this according to god's commandment to the Jews. **The search for the leaven is so arduous**, that not only do they thoroughly sweep, wipe, scrub, clean, mop, and disinfect their property, but they, the faithful Jews, **go to their hands and knees, crawling about the floor with lights**, searching out every nook and cranny for possible remnants of leaven. **These are facts** that all traditional Jews will readily admit to - with pride! Any leaven that is found or any articles that are found that may be *infected* with leaven are

Section One

The Secret Origins Of Judaism

taken to the outdoors, and in accordance with godly decree, burned to ashes - complete incineration is required.

All articles and utensils that may have been touched by leaven or contain any portion of leaven from the previous year must be removed from the premises, or in some cases *super-cleaned or flamed* by a special ritualistic process certified by the Rabbis. This includes any and all cooking utensils and dishes etc that were used by the family during the course of the previous year - all must be removed. **Special or reserved cooking and eating utensils**, that have not been previously used during the year (therefore not exposed to leaven) are brought out or bought for use during the Passover season. **Any food stuffs**, can goods, drinks, what have you, that have or may have the tiniest content of leaven, even 1/60th part of the whole must be removed from the premises.

The Jews are instructed to eat matzo for the seven days of the Hag Hamatzah, that is, the Feast of Unleavened Bread[2]. Matzo is a bread or cracker made without the use of leaven. The rationale given for this, is that the release of the Jews from Egypt was done in great haste - once the Egyptians agreed to release the Israelites they (the Egyptians) demanded that they exit quickly. Therefore, according to Judaic tradition, they (the Jews) did not have time to leaven their bread but had to prepare it quickly without leaven.

Also, the Jews are instructed, allegedly in compliance with divine decree, to eat the Passover lamb in great haste, with staff in hand, perhaps standing at the ready. **And all of the lamb must be eaten**, completely consumed - no leftovers are allowed according to the godly injunction; and if perchance there are leftovers, these **leftovers are to be incinerated**, that is, burned to

---

[2] **Leviticus 23:6** And on the fifteenth day of the same month *is* the feast of unleavened bread unto the LORD: seven days ye must eat unleavened bread.

Section One

The Secret Origins Of Judaism

ashes - made as the dust of the earth[3]. Again, the rationale for this is attributed to the great haste in which they were forced by the Egyptians to leave Egypt.

As to the preparation of the Passover lamb, it must be roasted over flame - it cannot be boiled, or broiled, baked, fried or cooked in any other way except by roasting over flame. It seems that god is very strict about these procedures. **It should be eaten with bitter herbs** is the biblical injunction.

The central part of the Passover observance is the sacramental meal called the Seder meal. This meal is intertwined with many strictly observed rituals. The complete procedure of Seder guidelines is explained in the Haggadah. **The Haggadah is the traditional text supplied to all participants** of the Seder so that all are held in conformity. The word Seder means *order* or *order of service*. **The rituals, foods, drinks, and utensils of the Seder table carry momentous symbolisms** pertaining to the *fabricated* history of the Jews, and their *fictitious* covenant with god. **It is a certainty** that the Seder observance has been constructed by the Rabbis so as to perpetuate the myth of the Jewish (Israelite) enslavement in Egypt, which, of course never actually occurred; likewise to systematically indoctrinate the Jewish flock, and imbue them with a sense of exceptionality and mission, to set them apart as a distinct and superior breed and to unify them. **The Egyptians show no records** of the events described in the bible and Quran relevant to the enslavement of Hebrews. In fact, when I was doing some research in Egypt some years ago, an Egyptologist told me that the ancient Egyptian economy and social system did not countenance slavery.

---

[3] **Exodus 12:8-10** And they shall eat the flesh in that night, roast with fire, and unleavened bread; *and* with bitter *herbs* they shall eat it. Eat not of it raw, nor sodden at all with water, but roast *with* fire; his head with his legs, and with the purtenance thereof. And ye shall let nothing of it remain until the morning; and that which remaineth of it until the morning ye shall burn with fire.

Section One

The Secret Origins Of Judaism

The settings of the Seder table are standard in all Jewish households, perhaps with minor regional adaptations; they include the Seder Plate - upon this plate are placed *a* **Zeroa** i.e. *Lamb Shank Bone,* representative of the Passover (lamb); a **Beitzah** i.e. *Roasted Egg,* symbol of the new life of spring and freedom on coming out from Egyptian slavery; **Maror** i.e. *Bitter Herbs,* said by the Jews to represent the bitterness of slavery; **Haroseth** i.e. mixture of *Chopped Apples, Nuts and Honey,* supposedly a symbol of the mortar that cements bricks together, to remind the Jews of the hard labor they endured while in bondage to the Egyptians; **Karpas** i.e. *Green Vegetable* such as parsley or lettuce, a symbol of green new life and consequently new hope for the longsuffering Jewish people; **Matzoth** i.e. a *3-layer stack of Matzoth* - this unleavened bread serves as a reminder of the quickness in which the Israelites had to flee Egypt; **also included in the menu** is **Salt Water** *or* as an alternative *Vinegar* - the salt water said to be a reminder of the tears that the Israelites shed in their suffering under the oppression of the Egyptians. **Cups of wine are on the table**, and a special place, cup or goblet is set in place for the expected prophet **Elijah** who is prophesied to come as a precursor for the **Jewish Messiah**.

The Seder service commences with a general blessing, followed by a ceremonial blessing befit for the occasion. Next the attendees wash their hands from a pitcher provided for the occasion; followed by each person dipping their green vegetable into the salt water before eating it, while uttering words of gratitude and thanks to god. At this time, the patriarch of the family removes the middle matzo and breaks it in two; he wraps the larger piece in a napkin or the like and hides it away - later, towards the end of the service, it will fall upon the children to search out the hidden matzo, now called the **Afikomen**, and present it to the family head for a recompense.

Attention is now turned to a discussion of the reasons for this gathering - a set order of questions and answers is prescribed in the Haggadah which

Section One

The Secret Origins Of Judaism

each person has at hand. The discussion involves the fictionalized[4] history of the Jews; their concocted heritage, the migration of their ancestors into Egypt, their noteworthy accomplishments there, their eventual enslavement, and cruel persecution by the Egyptians, their specialness in the eyes of god, their deliverance by god from bondage to the Pharaoh, and their binding covenant with god and on and on. After the discussions, and chanting, and singing, and so forth they turn their attention back to the Seder meal.

Again they ritualistically wash (cleanse) their hands from the pitcher, at the table, provided for the occasion - and another worshipful blessing is recited. The patriarch then recites another prayer or blessing over the matzoth, and forthwith distributes portions of the blessed bread to the assembled. Each attendee now prepares for oneself a *Hillel Sandwich*, a combination of the *Bitter Herbs*, the *Haroseth* (mixture of chopped apples, nuts, and honey) sandwiched in between the matzoth.

Finally, it's time to eat the grand meal! The assembled all dig in to a sumptuous feast, and I assume, with all the banter and joyful interaction that generally accompanies such occasions. **By the time everyone has become satiated**, someone from among the children has found the Afikomen that was hidden away earlier - and thus comes to the Patriarch to present the *find* for payment or a ransom (bargain) for some desired compensation - an agreement is reached; and the retrieved Afikomen is shared amongst all the assembled.

At closing another prayer or blessing is recited, possibly over wine, and tributes are made to Elijah, the expectant forerunner to the Messiah - the event closes.

---

[4] Of course many Jews take their fabled history very seriously

Section One

The Secret Origins Of Judaism

Linkage of Judaism To Its Primordial Semitic Origins

The Jewish Passover observance did not begin in tandem with the emancipation of the Jews from slavery in Egypt. The biblical story of Israel's enslavement by Egyptians is not verifiable through secular research - the story is religious dogma, not historical truth. The Passover festival or its like was in force among the Semitic people long before Judaism became an established religion, and long before the Hebrews became distinct, as a group, from other Semitic people. **The origins** of the *primordial core* of the Passover ritual, by whatever name it was anciently called, goes far back into prehistory, so far back that we cannot, with assurance, assign an era to its initiation. Far, far back into prehistorical times when mankind was in the embryonic stages of tribal or societal community development; whether or not from a status of environmental recovery or aboriginal initiation is an issue that may be discussed under another cover.

The religious reasons given for the observance of the Jewish traditions that we have penned above are clearly made-up fictions. The rituals themselves are clearly ludicrous, and that their sanction has been assigned to god is an abominable absurdity. **Think of it** - the Jews claim that god instructed them to sacrifice animals before him, and splatter the blood of these animals upon the entranceways to their homes; to run amuck in their Temples waving the first fruit of the harvest into the air as a dedication to the deity. I think it must be palpably clear to any rationally thinking person that these religious rites, without doubt, spring from *primal superstitions*. **Our task**, in which we are now actively engaged, is to link the Jewish traditions with their primitive core, which (core) has no genuine connection with religion, as we now perceive religion, nor with any cogent, coherent, realistic concept of god.

There is no <u>obvious</u> connection between the primal core of Judaism and the religion itself - **it is an *arcane* connection that must be explained in order to be understood**, but once the connection is explained, it becomes, to the average intellect, as clear as the brightest day. **A good analogy** is the seed (core) at the center of a fruit, such as a peach. Break open the peach

Section One

The Secret Origins Of Judaism

and reveal the seed (core) and there is absolutely no visible resemblance or similarity between the seed (core) and the flesh of the peach. Of course there is and has to be an innate connection, because the seed is the source from which the peach has grown, but in order for us to understand the *mechanics* of this indisputable seminal relationship we may need the input of an horticulturist, someone trained in the science of growing fruits and vegetables, to help us acquire a correct understanding .

It has been concluded, as evinced by our research, that the rituals and traditions observed or performed within Hebrew religion, have, in fact, evolved from pagan rituals practiced by primitive pre-Judaic Semites; and further, that Judaism, as we know it today, is an outgrowth of that primal core. Our task at hand, of course, is to present persuasive evidences in support of the aforesaid conclusion.

All of the Judaic *core* **religious rituals** originated **primitively** under Environmental Mythology, at a time when Man lacked an intellectual understanding of his natural environment and consequently sought to appease and/or bargain with the unknown spiritual forces that He imagined controlled the changes in his natural surroundings.

As Man developed intellectually over the passing generations He began to modify his rituals or festivals somewhat, **but more importantly** *the priests also modified the explanations* given to the public for the observance of the various festivals. This was done in reflection of a higher awareness of the causes of nature's vicissitudes. **In addition**, as religion evolved, the priesthood modified the explanations of religious traditions so as to indicate, falsely I might add, a innate religious connection to various cultural traditions that, in truth, *preceded* the formation of religion.

The important thing to remember is that the rituals preceded organized religion, and the ostensible explanations or overt interpretations of the rituals and their suggested meanings, as advocated by the Semitic priesthood, were *adapted* as a fit for the ensuing religious beliefs as the religious culture developed over the generations. **The Semitic priesthood invented the Egyptian slave tale** as a cultural explanation for the ancient

Section One

The Secret Origins Of Judaism

Spring Festival Rituals that they and others had been practicing for many generations, going back into pre-history.

It is of the highest importance to understand that as ancient primordial society became more *learned* over the generations, that this *learning* was *restricted* to a tiny, small fraction of the population, at the upper echelons of primitive societies. Even when writing developed anciently, writing was a tool of the ruling class - the masses were totally illiterate. **Of course, the primordial core of Judaism that we are now reviewing goes far back, even further than the development of writing.** But nevertheless, it is important to understand that when the rulers or the elite, so to speak, of the primordial masses sought to convey to the hordes some important *technical* or *intricate* societal message, they could not convey that message intellectually, through a group discussion of pertinent facts, as we might do today. **The ignorance of the masses was too absolute** for deliberative discussions in those long ago primordial ages. Rather they would finagle, coerce, manipulate, or maneuver the people through various contrivances, rituals, customs, and traditions so as to accomplish whatever goal the tribal elite had decided was necessary for the welfare of the tribe as a whole. Of course this system carries on, even today, as some of us know.

When the primitive rituals were originally enacted amongst the primal populations eons ago, the underlings may not have been aware, at all, of the *true* underlying factors that caused their leadership (priests or the equivalent) to enact certain rituals. They were given spurious explanations that suited there perceptive *capabilities* and *inclinations*. Even today, there are isolated pockets of people in various parts of the world that hang on to old primitive customs (strange rituals, dietary, sacrificial, sexual rites, self flagellation, dances, costumes, etc) going back untold years, and they are not able to give a rational explanation for the origin of their traditions, nor can they express a cogent explication of the symbolisms.

So what is the authentic <u>primitive origin</u> of the Judaic Passover tradition! What actually *is* the original and underlying meaning of the Jewish rituals conducted during Passover? In keeping with my previous

Section One

The Secret Origins Of Judaism

references to a primordial *dissimilar core* as the matrix from which Jewish and other religious traditions have evolved - what is that *primal, Semitic core* over which the Judaic Passover religious rituals have been overlaid? **The revealing** *Key* is in one word, although I will most certainly use more than just one word in my unveiling of this primordial symbolism - that word is *Sanitation*. **Within the context** of this expansive exposition, **Sanitation is defined** as the institutionalization of systems and procedures by which infectious diseases may be avoided or remedied enacted by the ancients, pursuant to the general welfare of a given group or community.

Within modern Judaism, the true practical reasons that the ancients conducted these traditions have been obscured from view; obscured under the veil of spurious explanations conveyed by the priesthood in regards to the true origin of the ritualistic activities that now take place during the Passover season. **These Jewish traditions, in truth, spring from an ancient annual hygienic system** of methodical *sanitization, decontamination* and *hygienic renewal*, conducted by the *pre-Judaic Semites* **annually**, after surviving the massive health perils commonly experienced and endured by primitive societies under the stark and dank conditions of the long winter sequestration. That is the veritable truth underlying the ludicrous misrepresentations foisted on us by the Jewish clergy.

We shall unveil the true underlying meanings of the Passover traditions shortly; **but first**, before we explain the instructive and innate connections between *systems of sanitation* and the traditional Passover rituals, **we must prove** that the ancient Semitic or Jewish leadership, the Rabbis, were aware of the perils inherent in a non-sanitary environment. **We must prove that the Rabbis knew and understood** that the lack of proper sanitation could possibly unleash various plagues upon their fledgling community, plagues so devastating so as to threaten the very survival of their nascent society.

The proofs are clearly expressed in the ancient Jewish chronicles at hand, that narrative called the *Torah*. **So we must presently defer to the Torah**, that is, the first five books of the bible for the proofs that the Rabbis

Section One

The Secret Origins Of Judaism

were keenly aware of the importance of sanitation to the welfare and survival of a given community, **and then**, after expounding on these proofs, **we will commence** the decoding of the Passover rituals relevant to systems of hygienic renewal.

Let us now review some passages in the bible *that are very important* to our subject. First off, let's use the bible to prove the symbiotic association, figuratively speaking, between *cleanliness* and *godliness*, so to speak. As I indicated above, the ancient Semites, that is to say the leadership, the sacerdotal class, was well aware of many factors not cognizant to the primitive masses of their societies; and one of those factors was knowledge of the importance of hygiene to the health and welfare of the general public. **Note the following biblical quotes that forcefully indicate how keenly aware of hygiene the Semites were**, and how systems of hygienic instructions were woven into Jewish tribal customs and given the sanction of god - please note that in the following verses god himself is the alleged instructor.

The verses are focused on measures to be taken in order to avoid contagion, contaminations, pathogen, and infectious diseases. **The original intent** of the rituals embodied in the Passover traditions had that exact same purpose - Sanitation. It was not until the Jewish Priests *invented* the fable about the Hebrew's Egyptian bondage that **they changed the interpretations of the traditions** so as to fit into the made-up tale about a divine legacy and godly covenant. I have *highlighted* and underlined some portions of these quotes for special emphases. **These biblical verses should be read with great diligence** as the information provided in them is crucial to the *interpretations* that we shall soon render.

Leviticus 15:1-5 **And the LORD spake** unto Moses and to Aaron, saying, Speak unto the children of Israel, and say unto them, When any man hath a running issue out of his flesh, because of his issue he is unclean. And this shall be **his uncleanness** in his issue: whether his flesh run with his issue, or his flesh be stopped from his issue, it is **his uncleanness**. Every bed, whereon he lieth that hath the issue, **is unclean**: and every thing, whereon he

Section One
37

The Secret Origins Of Judaism

sitteth, shall be unclean. And whosoever toucheth his bed shall wash his clothes, and bathe himself in water, and be unclean until the even.

Leviticus 15:13 And when he that hath an issue is cleansed of his issue; then **he shall number to himself seven days for his cleansing**, and wash his clothes, and bathe his flesh in running water, and **shall be clean**.

Leviticus 15:16-19 And if any man's seed of copulation go out from him, then he **shall wash all his flesh in water**, and be unclean until the even. And every garment, and every skin, whereon is the seed of copulation, **shall be washed with water**, and be unclean until the even. The woman also with whom man shall lie with seed of copulation, **they shall both bathe themselves in water**, and be unclean until the even. And if a woman have an issue, and her issue in her flesh be blood, **she shall be put apart seven days:** and whosoever toucheth her shall be unclean until the even.

Leviticus 7:19 And the flesh that toucheth any unclean thing shall not be eaten; it shall be burnt with fire: and as for the flesh, all that be clean shall eat thereof.

Leviticus 7:23-24 Speak unto the children of Israel, saying, Ye shall eat no manner of fat, of ox, or of sheep, or of goat. And the fat of the beast that dieth of itself, and the fat of that which is torn with beasts, may be used in any other use: but ye shall in no wise eat of it.

Leviticus 7:26 Moreover ye shall eat no manner of blood, whether it be of fowl or of beast, in any of your dwellings.

Leviticus 11:33-35 **And every earthen vessel**, whereinto any of them[dead animal] falleth, whatsoever is in it shall be unclean; and ye shall break it. Of all meat which may be eaten, that on which such water cometh shall be unclean: and all drink that may be drunk in every such vessel shall be unclean. And every thing whereupon any part of their carcase falleth shall be unclean; **whether it be oven, or ranges for pots, they shall be broken down: for they are unclean**, and shall be unclean unto you.

Section One

The Secret Origins Of Judaism

Leviticus 14:37-40 **And he shall look on the plague**, and, behold, if the plague be in the walls of the house with hollow strakes, greenish or reddish, which in sight are lower than the wall; Then the priest shall go out of the house to the door of the house, and shut up the house **seven days**: And the priest shall come again the seventh day, and shall look: and, behold, **if the plague be spread** in the walls of the house; Then the priest shall command that they take away the stones in which the plague is, and they shall cast them into an unclean place without the city:

Leviticus 15:13 And when he that hath an issue is cleansed of his issue; then he shall **number to himself** seven days **for his cleansing**, and wash his clothes, and bathe his flesh in running water, and shall be clean.

Numbers 19:11 He that toucheth the dead body of any man shall be unclean seven days.

Leviticus 3:17 It shall be a perpetual statute for your generations throughout all your dwellings, that ye eat neither fat nor blood.

Leviticus 13:31-33 And if the priest look on the plague of the scall, and, behold, it be not in sight deeper than the skin, and that there is no black hair in it; then the priest shall **shut up him that hath the plague of the scall seven days**: And in the seventh day the priest shall look on the plague: and, behold, if the scall spread not, and there be in it no yellow hair, and the scall be not in sight deeper than the skin; He shall be shaven, but the scall shall he not shave; and the priest shall shut up him that hath the scall seven days more:

Numbers 31:23 **Every thing that may abide the fire**, ye shall make it go through the fire, and it shall be clean: nevertheless it shall be purified with the water of separation: and **all that abideth not the fire** ye shall make go through the water.

I'm sure you noticed in this selective assortment of biblical passages that I have provided for your perusal that the single salient theme that permeates almost all of the verses is *avoidance of contagion*. **The importance** of washing is expressed, and the importance of *running water* for cleansing as

Section One

The Secret Origins Of Judaism

opposed to standing water is indicated. **The avoidance** of putrefied flesh is stipulated. **Sterilization by fire** or burning is recommended. **The people are directed to remove contaminated articles** from their premises to locations outside of the community so as to avoid the plague of infectious disease. **Quarantine is a constant theme** - it is evident that they viewed seven days as a minimum period of isolation, abstention, or restraint when dealing with items, people, or circumstances where the presence of contagion was indicated. **These health related injunctions** are ascribed to god as the author, but of course we know that these instructions were, in truth, composed by the **Jewish priesthood**.

As I have indicated several times in my writings, one of the primary purposes for the institution of ancient rituals and traditions was *instruction*. **The ancient priests were the masters** of their societies whether formally recognized as such or not. They were the spiritual leaders, the doctors, the social-legal advisers in terms of tribal laws and customs, counselors to the royalty, astronomers, mathematicians, scribes, teachers, agriculturists - they directed when to plant and harvest as ordained by the gods (stars). **The priesthood controlled** the destiny of their communities, and they employed great cunning in directing this destiny.

If they determined that a certain course of action should be incorporated into the fabric of the society, they simply *introduced an instruction in the form of ritual* that must be done at specified intervals as an obligation to the gods. **They**, as the mediators between the unseen spirits, gods or various iconic deities **could direct** the populace in any direction of their choosing through the inauguration of customs and traditions; customs and traditions that would survive after many millennia, although the understanding of why the traditions were practiced might die out after only a few generations. **Such was the situation** with the Passover traditions that we shall now commence translating.

The symbolisms of the seven Jewish feasts reflect two separate Semitic cultures that over time merged into one culture, and spawned Judaism or perhaps I should say Judaic culture; that is, according to some scholars that

Section One

The Secret Origins Of Judaism

have researched these issues down through the years. **The biblical Judaic culture thus reflects the integration** of nomadic Semites and Agrarian Semites. This is why we see in Judaic traditions, within the same framework, rituals on the one hand related to blood sacrifice, that of nomadic shepherds and hunters; while on the other hand, traditions related to grain offerings and harvest festivals.

The Passover Symbolisms

As regards the Passover sacrificial blood offering of the unblemished lamb, and the smearing of the lamb's blood upon the entranceway to the Hebrew homes, thus giving god a sign to *Pass Over* those blood stained dwellings during his death march through Egypt - the smearing of blood by ancient primitives on their bodies and property was extremely widespread in primordial times. Please refer to the book the *Golden Bough* by *James Frazer* - use the index for subject references and you will find copious information on this and similar methods of blood sacrificial customs among ancient primitives throughout the world. The ancient Semites were engaged in blood sacrifice and the smearing of blood at and about the entranceway to their dwellings long before the Egyptian story was concocted. But the cunning of the priesthood was such, that as they commenced the formulation of the Judaic religion some 2 1/2 to 3 millennia ago (according to various researches) they sought to assimilate the old Semitic customs into the newly formed or forming Judaic religion, consequently they made up the story about god's death march and the accompanying *pass over* the Jewish dwellings.

As we have indicated before, most festivals track the movement of the sun throughout the four cardinal points during the course of the tropical year. **Each time the sun makes a turn**, so to speak, (turns being indicated, of course, by the crossing of a cardinal point) the ancients would note that turn with some type of event, festival, sacrifice, what have you, that was appropriate to the occasion. The *Passing Over* signaled by the Passover feast was the sun's passing over the vernal equinox from the lower hemisphere into the northern hemisphere.

Section One

The Secret Origins Of Judaism

You will note that according to the biblical instruction, the Jews were instructed to eat the lamb in great haste and *none was to be left over*, and perchance if some was left over, *it was not to be consumed* but rather *burned to ashes*. **This was prescribed** in order *to avoid the consumption of putrefied meat*, and the inevitable sickness that would have resulted from such consumption.

They did not have refrigeration, and the sacrificial meat of the Passover had not been preserved by any of the ancient methods - it was killed on the evening of the 14th and consumed that same evening. **The biblical instruction stated** that at the dawn of the next day all of the meat *must be consumed or destroyed* - this is clearly a health advisory, nothing spooky or religious about it when looked at through the lens of rationality.

Also, according to biblical decree, the meat had to be prepared over *open flame* - no other method was acceptable; this is emphasized in Exodus 12:8-10. **This method, again, was because of sanitary concerns** - the best way to assure that there would be no cross-contamination from infected utensils was by open flame cooking, plus open fire was the *hottest* way of assuring that the meat was well cooked so as to minimize the possibilities of harmful bacteria infecting and surviving in the meat.

The religious misapplications foisted by the priesthood, which are so nonsensical, about eating in haste so as to avoid the marauding Egyptian armies, is really laughable when you think about it. **The Jewish priesthood made this story up** so that an old tradition (blood sacrifice) would be made to fit into their new religious culture, now called Judaism.

Feast Of Unleavened Bread Symbolisms

As regards the Feast Of Unleavened Bread, one of the most significant aspects about this agrarian festival is the preparation made the night before the 15th of Nisan when the faithful Jews go to *extraordinary and extreme* ends to assure that no leaven remains in their houses when Passover arrives. **Again, the explanation given to us by the Rabbis** for this fanatical undertaking is near total if not total nonsense. The Rabbis once again come

Section One

The Secret Origins Of Judaism

up with this story about leaving Egypt in great haste, thereby not having time to bake bread with leaven. **But even if this were the case**, that is to say, *the rapid exit scenario* - what has that to do with the faithful Jews crawling on their hands and knees with lights in an effort to assure that no leaven remains anywhere on their premises during Passover season? **How can the rapid exit of Egypt** be *intelligently* reconciled with the commencement of a tradition that demands a fanatical dread of leaven for seven days out of the 365 day year? **This is not rational**, and the reason that it's not rational is because the entire story of a rapid exit from Egypt is a misrepresentation.

This farcical story of leaving Egypt in great haste and therefore not being able to leaven the bread **was concocted** by the Rabbis to give a make-do explanation for a ritual that *was already in place* among the Semites, long before Judaism was formulated as a religion. The preparation of Matzoth (unleavened bread) goes back anciently amongst the Semitic people, that is for those Semitic tribes that were agrarians, farmers. **This is because** harvesting was a hectic affair that had to be done quickly, by large groups of non-residents or immigrants ingathered to the harvest sites and living in temporary dwellings. **It was customary** for those tribes, during the *massive influx* of peoples during the harvest seasons, **to prepare food quickly**, hence Matzoth were prepared during those temporary periods of *congestion* and *frenzy*. **The Rabbis needed a way** to assimilate into the evolving Jewish religion a tradition that was *already extant and ingrained* in the population, **therefore they invented** the Egyptian saga of *Slavery* and *Exodus*, and inserted the Passover and Unleavened Bread customs, that were already established traditions at the time, into a Judaic religious context - it was and is a great deception.

Section One

The Secret Origins Of Judaism

Another factor that truly exposes the idiocy of the Exodus scenario - the bible asserts that the Hebrews that exited Egypt numbered 600,000[5] souls plus livestock etc. Can you imagine the prodigious sanitation, logistical and communication problems attendant to transferring over a half million people quickly, on a moments notice, *to no where in particular*, just *out* of the land of Egypt - into the desert. And this amount of people allegedly wandering for forty years in the desert, living on bread[6] dropped from the skies. It truly baffles me that intelligent people take these religious assertions of the Jews seriously - but I digress.

The true reason for the seven day ban of leaven is Sanitation, the elimination of possible contagion - again, I must repeat for emphases, there is nothing mysterious or religious about this *leaven ritual* when it is properly decoded and unglued from its religious veneer.

Think of it - for 358 days of the year, leaven is heartedly welcomed and cherished, but for 7 days out of the year this same leaven is shunned and abhorred as if it were the *harbinger of the plague*! **Well, to tell the truth, that was actually the case** - potentially, the aged leaven[7] (sourdough) was, in fact, if contaminated, **a carrier of pathogens** or infectious disease. **And the potential for the spreading of infectious disease explains** the fanaticism of the ancients in removing every remnant of leaven from their homes during the *annual 7-day period of hygienic renewal*, now called by modern Jews, in keeping with an ultra religious flare for the holiday season, Hag Hamatzah or *Feast Of Unleavened Bread.*

---

[5] **Exodus 12:37-38** And the children of Israel journeyed from Rameses to Succoth, about six hundred thousand on foot *that were* men, beside children. And a mixed multitude went up also with them; and flocks, and herds, *even* very much cattle.

[6] **Exodus 16:35** And the children of Israel did eat manna forty years, until they came to a land inhabited; they did eat manna, until they came unto the borders of the land of Canaan.

[7] Explanations on the linkage between leaven and sourdough will be given as our essay progresses

Section One

The Secret Origins Of Judaism

Also, the fact that this adverseness toward leaven comes right at the end of winter, as the sun makes the turn toward spring holds great significance that we shall explore as our essay unfolds.

It is important that one divorces oneself from *present era thinking*, and tries to *imagine the living conditions and mindset of the primitives* so many millennia ago when these customs were formulated. **During the winters of those bygone days, the population was cooped up in primitive dwellings with earthen floors**, no running water, damp and putrid, along with myriad insects, mice, and whatever. So right after this winter sequestration, the priests customarily demanded, in the name of a deity, spirit or god, that the pre-Judaic Semites thoroughly clean their dwellings so as to assure that their deities (by whatever names they were then called) not be offended or angered by the presence of leaven during a special seven day interval. Could this be a subterfuge, enacted by the wily priesthood, pursuant to forced spring cleaning and the consequent improved sanitation? I think so.

The method utilized by the priesthood of compelling unlearned and brutish primitives, *by the command of god,* to fanatically and ritualistically clean their residences during an annual ritual, was much more effective than perhaps attempting an intelligent dialogue with the somewhat dullard masses of that time. **I'm sure the priests would not have gained the required cooperation** if they had requested the cleaning *with an attempted explanation* of the possibilities of virulent disease epidemics more readily facilitated under noxious, unsanitary conditions. The common classes probably would not have accepted or recognized the connection between sanitation and health in those bygone days. This is, in fact, a practical, rational observation that has been overlooked in regards to the Leaven related hysteria, amongst the Jews, concomitant with the Passover season.

One thing is certain, it is totally absurd to accept the idea that the presence of leaven in one's house during one particular week of the year amounts to an abominable sin against god. The populace was instructed to fanatically clean their homes in an effort to assure that leaven was not present; also to roast their meat over open flames only, *and to burn not stow any leftovers -*

Section One

The Secret Origins Of Judaism

this surely reads like an effort to avert the possible spread of disease that is directly associated with contagion. It is certain that the ancients, after living two to three months in forced winter sequestration, in darkness or only meager lighting, in dampness; stifling, putrid air; myriad vermin, unwashed, with unchanged clothing *plastered* to their bodies - that these poor souls were an exceedingly miserable lot when the weather broke and they were able to break loose from such confinement.

I believe that the explanation that I have rendered for the *true origin* of the Passover, and Feast Of Unleavened Bread festivals is reasonable and persuasive! **The historical and circumstantial evidence is, indeed overwhelming,** that at the core, these festivals (which in essence serve to denote the coming of Spring, as the sun passes over the vernal equinox) have no realistic spiritual significance. Hence we can reasonably and justifiably conclude, with supreme confidence, that these ritual activities do not, in fact, elevate the practitioners into a higher relationship with an existent deity - the activities are the continuation of old primitive rituals under a modern religious guise.

This is a very important factor: the ancient Semites used sourdough to leaven their bread - **they did not use modern style leaven such as baking soda.** Sourdough is produced by simply adding water to flour and allowing it to set to itself at room temperature. This combination of water and milled grain instigates the growth of bacteria in short duration, and this bacterial fermentation has the effect of leaven. **When the ancients desired to leaven their bread**, they took a portion (a *lump* as biblically expressed) of the sourdough and added it to a fresh bread mix. This system of using *lumps* of sourdough as leaven is practiced to this day, in some old style bakeries, so I am told.

The leaven (sourdough) was maintained by the ancients day to day, week to week, month to month, by adding fresh flour and water as needed to maintain the desired quantity. Through this ancient leavening process, that is to say, using lumps of sourdough to leaven the bread, the same batch of dough was used indefinitely. The same core batch would be used, by

Section One

The Secret Origins Of Judaism

additions, *for the entire year or years* unless the process was broken, and a new batch initiated - but the process was never broken! At some point, we don't know exactly when, the ancient Semitic priesthood, that is to say, the pre-Judaic priests or clerics, by whatever title they were called before Judaism came into its own, decided to interrupt the custom - clearly in the interest of sanitation. The priests initiated a new tribal tradition that required the complete removal of sourdough (leaven) from the premises for a period of seven days annually - such was the primordial origin of the *Feast of Unleavened Bread festival* or its equivalent.

We can be sure that the 7-day period was a quarantine because the biblical verses that we reviewed earlier in the essay clearly indicated the use of a *7-day quarantine* in combating contagion and infectious diseases. So it is quite evident from the evidence that we have presented that the Feast of Unleavened Bread as well as the Passover festival, under whatever pre-Judaic titles these feasts may have been originally labeled, that *both* preceded the formation of the Judaic religion among the Semitic people.

As Judaism was being formulated and established among the Semitic tribes, it behooved the priest to incorporate a method of assimilation for the traditions extant among the Semites. The story about not being able to leaven their bread because of a hasty exit out of Egypt is not credible, especially since the Hebrews were never slaves to the Egyptians, but beyond that - how not having time to bake with leaven could translate into a festival that demands the fanatical removal of leaven from the household is totally incompatible.

I think that it is beyond rational doubt that the true reason that the ancients instituted a 7-day ban on leaven, that is, sourdough was to prevent the possible spread of pathogens. **Clearly, the Jewish leadership was aware** of the potential health hazards of noxious, unsanitary surroundings, in association with years-old sourdough (leaven) and other household filth. **Some activities historically common among Jews during the Passover season**, such as bonfires for the burning of the leaven and other potential health contaminants, *clearly indicate* extreme efforts to avert the onslaught

Section One

The Secret Origins Of Judaism

of contagious disease and plague brought on by poor sanitation, which inevitably accompanied the long sequestration of winter among the primordial Semites. **The traditional practice of the Semites in boiling their cooking utensils,** and *burning* metal cookeries till they were red hot as a means of sterilization or sanitization *all confirm efforts to combat potential contagion and pathogens.*

And above all, we must remember, to the benefit of our own personal edification and better understandings **this key point:** that the *original* incentives that spawned all or nearly all of these ancient rituals, that have come down to us through the ages, were related to Man's attempts to contend, appease, or ameliorate the potentially adverse or hostile forces within the environment. **It is an undeniable fact that Practical, mundane causes and purposes laid beneath the overtly spiritual, ritualistic traditions of the ancient Hebrews.** So we must lend reasonable consideration to the practical *result* that accompanied the ritualistic and unusually zealous campaign to eliminate all, absolutely all leaven from the environs of the community - and *that result* was a spectacular Spring Cleaning pursuant to a more healthful environment.

Actually rigorous spring cleaning or renewal, if you will, was a widespread tradition on into the 20th century, even among the industrial nations. **Just a few decades ago it was common**, at the dawn of spring, to throw open the houses, pull out the rugs, sheets, and covers and beat the winter dust out of them; to fanatically clean and air out the houses, dispose of accumulated old clothing and what have you. **Just think** and imagine how *intensified* this procedure must have been thousands of years ago when people were cooped up throughout the winter in tents, caves, huts, and mud-brick dwellings, with no windows; living with rats, mice, bugs, lice and all manner vermin, with no running water or modern heat facilities. **Many of our inherited cultural traditions** were *configured* and *birthed* in those ancient eras, *influenced* and *shaped* by the conditions and environment of those long ago times.

Section One

The Secret Origins Of Judaism

The Seder Symbolisms

As regards the Seder observance, which, as we know, is the center point of the Jewish Passover festival - this service is, admittedly, very ritualistic, with multiple symbolisms offered as reflections of the alleged Hebrew experience as settlers, then as slaves in Egypt; and finally caped off with their divine deliverance by the direct intervention of god. **Of course there is absolutely no credible evidence** that the Hebrew experience in Egypt as depicted in the bible ever took place. **So in consequence of this fact**, it is quite obvious that the Seder symbolism must, in truth, have other underlying interpretations, other than those broadcasted by the Jews. **The task before us is to unveil those hidden symbolisms**, that heretofore have been obscured by an insidious religious facade.

The true, authentic origin of the Seder tradition is consistent with the overall focuses of the Passover season, as we have shown above, that is, in a word - Sanitation. And again, in keeping with the context of our expose' into the true origins of the Passover traditions, we define Sanitation renewal as *the institutionalization of systems and procedures by which infectious diseases may be avoided or remedied* pursuant to the general welfare of a given group or community.

A brief description of the Seder event is in the following. I need not give a detailed account of the *traditional* Seder service, since the observance was previously explained in a prior portion of our essay.

The Seder Service begins with Kiddush which is a ceremonial blessing, **next** the serving of wine, **a ceremonial washing** of hands. **Parsley is dipped** in salt water before eating. **Patriarch breaks** one of 3 matzoth in half, wraps it in napkin and hides it. **Wine is served** a 2nd time, **asking of the 4 questions** - from children about the reasons for the festival, **general discussion** of the Egyptian saga etc. A book known as the **Haggadah** is used to assure conformity to all of the rituals.

Traditional Jewish Seder interpretations

Salt water = tears of suffering Jews

Section One

The Secret Origins Of Judaism

Haroseth (mixed apples, honey and nuts) = the mortar for the Egyptian buildings

Karpas (green vegetable) Spring of the year

Shank bone (symbol of the sacrificial lamb)

Egg = source of life

Bitter Herbs + bitterness of slavery

Matzoth = Unleavened Bread

Items on Seder Menu

Traditionally, there are six items on the Seder plate as follows:

Shank bone

Roasted egg

Green vegetable such as parsley, lettuce

Matzoth

Bitter herbs

Mixed nuts and apples, in honey

Also included on the table: Salt water, a Pitcher of Water, and Wine

Seder Process

Dipping vegetable into salt water

Breaking middle matzo

Four questions from children, described as intelligent, rebellious, retarded, shy - telling the Exodus story (Haggadah)

Eating of the matzo, bitter herbs, Haroseth, and the serving of dinner

The Secret Origins Of Judaism

Finding the Afikomen by the children, and presenting it for a ransom payment

Opening of the door in quest of the expected Elijah

As indicated above the Rabbis have offered various puerile interpretations for the symbolisms of the Seder table. **It is quite evident that the meanings given to us by the Jewish priests are make-do explanations**, in an effort to fit pre-Judaic rituals into a modern religious context; and really quite haphazardly contrived in my opinion. The explanations of the symbolisms are suitable for children and their mental equivalents, but not for those of perceptive intellects.

We are told by the Rabbis that the <u>salt water</u> symbolizes the tears of the longsuffering Hebrews while in bondage to the Egyptians; that the <u>Haroseth</u> is symbolic of the mortar they were forced to laboriously mix by their Egyptian taskmasters; that the <u>Karpas</u> i.e. green vegetable indicates the greenness of the season in which they were liberated and the fresh hope of the spring season; that the <u>shank bone</u> was a symbol of the Passover itself; that the <u>egg</u> was a symbol of new birth as all new life comes from an egg of some sort; that the <u>bitter herbs</u> are a symbol of the bitterness of slavery.

The <u>true origin</u> of certain symbols at the Seder table are inalterably connected to systems of sanitation and hygiene pursuant to the avoidance and remediation of infectious diseases or contagion. Some other Seder symbols are connected with the passing over of the sun from the lower hemisphere of winter and darkness into the upper hemisphere of spring and light. The Rabbis have simply supplanted the sun under the type of Israel and concocted the story of Israel's enslavement to Egypt so as to signify the liberation of the Hebrew people instead of the true symbolism which, of old, pointed to the sun, that is the liberation of the sun from the winter underworld of bondage when it *passed over* the vernal equinox into the cosmic north - a transition that was symbolically equated with the liberation of the sun.

Section One

The Secret Origins Of Judaism

In regards to the Salt Water, Jewish literature on the Seder service reveals that some Jews substitute vinegar for the salt water. This is fine, because vinegar fits the symbolism just as splendidly as salt water. **The ancients used two natural disinfectants or sanitizing agents,** one was salt water and the other was vinegar. <u>The fact that salt water is a disinfectant explains the Seder ritual of dipping the green vegetable into the salt water so as to sanitize it.</u>

The Bitter Herbs were actually cathartic herbs designed to *clean the system*. The first action taken, anciently, in fighting disease was to purge the system, clean the system; so that is why they used cathartics (bitter herbs) during this seven days season of hygienic renewal. In fact some of us who are older probably remember that when we were coming up years ago that our parents still used the tactic of purging the system when we, as children became ill. I can remember the horrible taste of castor oil to this day.

In regards to the Matzoth, we reviewed that above, and we know that the reason for eating the matzoth during the Seder and the continued seven days of the Passover season, in lieu of regular bread, was <u>in order to avoid possible bacterial contamination from old sourdough i.e. leaven</u>. And, of course, the seven-day prohibition functioned as a quasi-quarantine, the period necessary to be assured that harmful bacterium or contagion was no longer active or potentially active.

In regards to the ceremonial washing of hands during the Seder service - of course we all should wash our hands before eating; however the washing of hands during the Seder service is not of the norm - it is ceremonial. The washing is done from a pitcher at the table at least twice at prescribed intervals during the service. I interpret these ceremonial washings (in their original context of eons ago) as symbols of required hygiene imposed on the primitives by the priesthood. Of course the Jews ascribe spiritual significance to the washings, which may be true in a present day religious context; but **our focus is on the origin of these symbols way back before Judaism took form as a religion**; <u>and I suggest that the original</u>

Section One

The Secret Origins Of Judaism

significance of these ceremonial washings was *Sanitation*., in keeping with the original ancient focus of the pre-Judaic Passover traditions.

As mentioned, there are, as standards, *six items* on the **Seder Plate** itself, which are the *Shank Bone*, the *Egg*, the *Green Vegetable*, the *Unleavened Bread*, the *Bitter Herbs*, and the *fruit-blend* consisting of honey, chopped apples, and Nuts. **Of these six items**, three symbolize the Cosmic Passover of the sun from the underworld into the upper regions, and three are indicative of hygienic concerns. The lamb's bone shows the sign of Aries at the vernal equinox, the Egg shows the rebirth or emergence of the sun as it surmounts the vernal equinox, and the Green vegetable shows the coming greenness of spring and summer. As noted above the Matzoth were eaten so as to avoid bread contaminated with old sourdough (leaven), and the Bitter Herbs were cathartic. As to the fruit blend, I have not been able to uncover or work out exact correlations - it may be a matter of nutrition.

We will come back to the Seder symbolism later in our series as we tie some of the interpretations into other aspects of the cultural mythology. **There are certain mystical symbolisms** to the Seder Plate, but I do not want to address those at this time. **We are focused** within this Section on proving the secular origins of the Jewish religious traditions, so we shall leave the unveiling of the mystical symbolisms for later.

Mythological Parallels Of The Passover Festival

Of course, in regard to the Passover traditions of the Jews, we have emphasized the *real life* environmental associations from which the various rituals were derived. **The ancient source or matrix of modern Judaic religious traditions is found** in the customs and rituals of primordial pagan Semites; and not in the alleged revelations or communications of god almighty to a chosen people. **Our primary focus** within this book is the unveiling of the *practical mundane inducements* that lay at the core of *all* cultural rituals; rituals derived from a prehistorical primordial core, that now in our day have become, in modified form, modern religious rituals and

Section One

The Secret Origins Of Judaism

traditions. **Originally, the rituals**, at the points of their inceptions, dealt with practical mundane matters associated with the *interactions of Man with his environment*; and *not* with spiritual or religious concerns. **That the spiritual-religious** aspect developed later, over generations, is my contention.

The modern rituals have been modified in terms of association - we now apply spiritual significance to rituals that originally, when anciently initiated, reflected the secular interaction of primitive Man with his environment. **The first symbolisms** or rituals employed by the aboriginals of the various regions of the planet, including the Semites, were *Environmentally* motivated at the most basic levels, in reflection of early Man's underdeveloped intellect. **Later, over the millennia**, as mankind's intellection expanded, in association with their vastly improved understanding and comprehension of the causative factors underlying the vacillations of nature, **then** mankind's symbolisms, as expressed in their rituals and myths, became much more sophisticated, and spiritual.

As I indicated earlier in the essay, when engaged in the process interpreting biblical and cultural mythology, **we must keep in mind** that there are two major or *parent* categories of mythology. **There is Environmental Mythology** which reflects mankind's earliest attempts to define his habitat, often laden with emotional, primitive superstitions; and also, **developing much later in time**, the category of **Scientific Mythology** which indicates, in its interpretations, a highly advanced understanding of the environmental sciences and the expanded cosmos.

Mythological symbolizations, when accurately interpreted, show distinct parallels at their varied levels of decipherment. **All levels of mythology parallel each other**, with only minor variations; variations usually reflective of cultural inputs. **Also**, all of the symbolizations (mythological stories) run in parallel to the *underlying physical realities* that were the original *patterns*, which the symbolisms copied, and reproduced symbolically in varied mythological stories, and/or ritualistic customs.

Section One

The Secret Origins Of Judaism

That's why, for example, the mythology of the Israelites emerging from bondage in Egypt at the dawn of spring, parallels the emergence of the sun from its seeming bondage in the celestial underworld at the same interval of time. **Likewise**, Noah's ark landed upon Mount Ararat[8] during the interval of the vernal equinox, thereby being safely secured above the raging waters below. **And**, in continued conformity, Jesus Christ was resurrected at the same interval, which is of course *Passover* or the sun's *passing over* vernal equinox.

All three of the aforementioned myths are mythological copies of the same underlying cosmic event, that is to say, the emergence of the sun from the lower cosmic hemisphere into the higher cosmic hemisphere at the crossing of the vernal equinox. **All three** of these major biblical symbolisms hover around the same astronomical event, and likewise possess the same identical theme of *Deliverance*, because **all three** mythological episodes are reflective of the same underlying reality, that is the sun ascending above the vernal equinox.

When the sun *crossed over* the vernal equinox, or, perhaps I should say, Passed Over the vernal equinox thus inducing the spring of the year, this *passing* marked the occasion of deliverance of the Israelites from bondage in Egypt. **In terms of astro-theological symbolism**, Israel symbolized the sun, so that astronomically the deliverance symbolically indicated the *emancipation of the sun* from its bondage in the underworld below the equinoxes. **Likewise**, our primitive ancestors were customarily held in bondage (sequestered) during the winter season. They lacked the resources to effectively contend with the climatic onslaught of winter, and in consequence were forced into seclusion for their survival's sake. **During their winter** hibernation, they endured conditions that were cold, damp, cramped, famishing, noxious, and confining. **Their primary food source**

---

[8] **Genesis 8:4** And the ark rested in the seventh month, on the seventeenth day of the month, upon the mountains of Ararat. --The 7th month of the Civil year is the 1st month of the Religious year, hence Nisan (Abib) 17, the 2nd day of Passover

Section One

The Secret Origins Of Judaism

was stowed grains and meats that they had secured when the sun was high. Not only was it necessary that they have sufficient quantities of food to last for three winter months, they also had to avoid *putrefaction* and/or *contamination* of their winter food supply.

The Passover season, that is to say the sun *passing over* the vernal equinox (which signaled the coming of spring), did actually *in real world terms* bring emancipation and freedom to the longsuffering primitives of primordial times. **In those bygone days** they lacked the resources and knowledge to successfully contend with the wraths of the overlords of winter. **Their only option** in those early days of mankind's aboriginal emergence was to wait out the storms of winter, until delivered by the savior sun at the dawn of spring. **We need to empathize**, seek to comprehend and *feel* the devastating impressions inculcated into the human consciousness and psyche of our primitive benighted ancestors by the *perils of winter*, and other oppressive forces of nature, **and also apprehend** that it was from this mix that our original spiritual concepts, as a species, were spawned.

We need to understand as best we can, that our present day religious concepts have not spontaneously materialized out of a vacuum, (and most certainly god did not compose these religious concepts) but rather the basic precepts that we have now refined into our current theological concepts, were originally cemented into the psyches of our primordial ancestors many eons ago. **We need** only to unwrap the layers of our cultural and religious veneers accumulated over the ages, to thereby unveil the primordial ancient core, the matrix, as it were, still intact.

Sacrifices of Lent

In regards to Lent, the 40-day Lent observance is alleged by some to imitate the Forty Days Temptation of Christ. **After Jesus was baptized** in the river Jordan, it is alleged that he was immediately taken to task by Satan - Satan desired to prevent his mission, as the story goes. At this same time, John The Baptist was imprisoned and subsequently beheaded; and of course,

Section One

The Secret Origins Of Judaism

Jesus prevailed over the temptations and commenced his one-year mission of teaching the gospels , culminating in his sacrificial death.

This biblical scenario is bursting with cosmic symbolism that begs to be explained. I have given an extensive explanation of the Forty-Day symbolism in *Book Two of The Astrological Foundation Of The Christ Myth*, so **at this point**, we need only explain the mythology or cosmic symbolism that is signified in the biblical tale which describes the transition from the ministry of *John The Baptist* to that of *Jesus The Christ*; and that we shall do in short order.

As regards the sacrificial death of Christ, it was deemed necessary because *god the father* thirsted for the blood of mankind to pay for the purported horrendous sin of Adam in the Garden of Eden i.e. the sin of disobedience in that Adam and Eve ate of the forbidden fruit. **The need of a Sacrificial Death** to pay for the sins of Man is doctrinal within Christianity. So someone came up with the idea, perhaps Jesus, or the Holy Ghost, or god the father himself, that in order to quench the bloodlust of god, a proxy would do just as well as the whole of mankind. In consequence of this, Jesus was designated as the Scapegoat that died for the sins of Adam and his seed.

Please note that the aforementioned is the foundation upon which Christianity has been established; that is to say, that Jesus Christ died for the sins of all mankind (Adam and his seed); **and also**, in addition, *the resurrection of Jesus from the grave* is presented as proof that Jesus was indeed the Son of god. **In consequence** we are told, that our *only* salvation is to accept Jesus Christ as our savior. And what shall belief in Jesus save us from? Well, belief in Jesus will save us from the wrath of god, because it is prophesied that god will kill all disbelievers on Judgment Day. But all those that escape the *killing fields* by reason of their faith in Jesus shall live forever with god, and never ever see death - this is the Christian doctrine in a nutshell. How rational, intelligent people can accept such a doctrine as divine is beyond me, but I digress.

In regards to the astro-theological symbolism, Jesus and John were polar opposites, whether at opposite ends of the equinoxes or opposite ends of the

Section One

The Secret Origins Of Judaism

solstices. Jesus was the sun at positive polarity and John was also the sun, *but at negative polarity*. **In this phase of the mythology**, the position of the sun as it breaks the horizon in the *east* is likened to *Jesus the Christ*, while the position of the sun at sunset in the *west* as it dives into the underworld sea is likened unto *John the Baptist*. **The bible sets the birth** of John proximate to the summer Solstice, and the birth of Jesus proximate to the winter solstice.

Of course popular tradition claims, *falsely*, that the birth of Jesus is not given in the bible, but that is not true - the birth of Jesus is given in Luke of the bible. The birth date of Jesus is inferred in Luke of the bible by reference to the cycles of the moon, and also by relations of the birth of Jesus to the birth of John as being separated by six months. **I have given a complete explanation of this** in chapter Two of *The Astrological Foundation Of The Christ Myth Book Three*. The birth date of John The Baptist is widely given as June 24, which is correct - his birth came three days after the summer solstice. Of course John is a myth and never actually existed as a human being, but as a symbol of the negative polarity of the sun, he (John) was born three days after the summer solstice on June 24.

The summer solstice is the highest point of the sun's annual cycle, but nevertheless it is termed *negative polarity* in this phase of the symbolism because of the sun's negative trajectory after crossing the summer solstice. The date of John's birth, i.e. three days after the summer solstice, marks the decline or fall of the sun from that high point to its (John the Baptist) eventual death at the winter solstice on December twenty-two. This is why, in the solar phase of the symbolism, the ancients wept for Tammuz[9], also a symbol of the sun, during a mourning period signaled by the decline of the

---

[9] **Ezekiel 8:14-16** Then he brought me to the door of the gate of the LORD'S house which *was* toward the north; and, behold, there sat women weeping for Tammuz. Then said he unto me, Hast thou seen *this*, O son of man? turn thee yet again, *and* thou shalt see greater abominations than these. And he brought me into the inner court of the LORD'S house, and, behold, at the door of the temple of the LORD, between the porch and the altar, *were* about five and twenty men, with their backs toward the temple of the LORD, and their faces toward the east; and they worshipped the sun toward the east.

Section One

The Secret Origins Of Judaism

sun from its apex, at the summer solstice. **Once the sun passes over** the summer solstice, it commences its descent toward the netherworld, and its fateful destiny is sealed. The sun, *as mythologically expressed*, will fall into imprisonment when it passes through the autumnal equinox into the forces of the cosmic underworld (symbolized as imprisonment), and after three more months will be executed while so imprisoned, at the point of the winter solstice.

The scenario for Jesus Christ is the Exact opposite of that applied to John The Baptist. Jesus is born three days after the winter solstice, as a symbol of the sun that is moving positively toward victory over the forces of the underworld. **Three months after his birth**, as the sun, he will pass over the vernal equinox and commence his (the sun's) mission to bring light and redemption to the beleaguered world, ravaged by the torments of winter.

Note the passage from John of the bible wherein John the Baptist speaks of his destiny: John 3:28-30 Ye yourselves bear me witness, that I said, I am not the Christ, but that I am sent before him. He that hath the bride is the bridegroom: but the friend of the bridegroom, which standeth and heareth him, rejoiceth greatly because of the bridegroom's voice: this my joy therefore is fulfilled. He must increase, but I must decrease.

John says of Jesus in the closing verse quoted above - *he must increase, but I must decrease*. This verse clearly reflects the opposite polarities of the sun as symbolized by John The Baptist and Jesus The Christ; seemingly two suns at opposite ends of a crosspiece in rotation, so that as the crosspiece rotates in its daily or annual cycle, the upward movement of the positive end by natural process brings downward rotation to the opposite end. **In reference to the present symbolism**, each day the sun moves so as to establish *two prominent positions* or coordinates in the sky, **that is** the

Section One

The Secret Origins Of Judaism

position of the *rising sun in the east* at positive polarity i.e. Jesus, and the position of the *setting sun in the west* at negative polarity i.e. John[10].

Note the following biblical verses from Mark of the bible: Mark 1:9-14 And it came to pass in those days, that Jesus came from Nazareth of Galilee, and was baptized of John in Jordan. And straightway coming up out of the water, he saw the heavens opened, and the Spirit like a dove descending upon him: And there came a voice from heaven, saying, Thou art my beloved Son, in whom I am well pleased. And immediately the Spirit driveth him into the wilderness. And he was there in the wilderness forty days, tempted of Satan; and was with the wild beasts; and the angels ministered unto him. Now after that John was put in prison, Jesus came into Galilee, preaching the gospel of the kingdom of god,

The symbolisms of the preceding verses are explicit and straightforward, and therefore quite easily interpreted. We have already established that Jesus and John represent opposite polarities of the sun, as the sun revolves around the earth[11], daily or annually; polarities imaginarily positioned at opposite ends of a rotating cosmic crosspiece, with the earth stationed at the center of the crosspiece. **In this phase of the symbolism**, with John and Jesus paired in representing the sun - the upward movement of the sun indicates Jesus, while the downward movement indicates John. **The river Jordan** is the line of connection between the equinoxes, with John positioned at the autumnal equinox, in decline, at the end of his mission as it were; and Jesus rising, at the commencement of his salvational mission at the vernal equinox. The word baptism, of course, signifies initiation, a new start, a turning point for the sun (Jesus) as it passes over the line of the equinoxes, symbolized in Mark as the river Jordan.

---

[10] The etymology of the word John indicates fish, Ioannes. This is significant because the western sun was thought to swim or sail through the underworld waters in some of the ancient symbolisms

[11] Of course the sun only apparently revolves around the earth. Ancient mythology was written so as to reflect the apparent movement of the sun.

Section One

The Secret Origins Of Judaism

I have enumerated the prominent factors of the solar[12] symbolism as presented in Mark of the bible: (1) Jesus and John together in the river Jordan which signifies the sun of both positive and negative polarities, at equipoise at the line of the vernal equinox (2) When Jesus (positive sun polarity) crosses above the equinox, he immediately enters into 40 days of trials with Satan (3) When John (Negative sun polarity) falls below the line of the equinoxes he is immediately imprisoned. I think that the symbolisms of Jesus and John as aspects of the solar sun, as expressed in Mark, are crystal clear. (1) Jesus the Christ and John The Baptist meet at the equinox line (2) when Jesus, as sun, passes over the vernal equinox, this movement commences the forty-day period of seasonal transition, depicted in Mark as trials with Satan (residual effect of winter) (3) at the same time that Jesus (eastern sun) combats Satan, John (western sun) is thrown into prison (the cosmic underworld).

Of course, our primary focuses, at this time, are the Judaic traditions; nevertheless I think I should add, in brief, some comments concerning the Christian observances of Lent, which also relate to the Passover season, that is the passing of the sun over the vernal equinox.

The Lent period is preceded by Shrovetide, which are a few days, according to modern customs, of raucous activities leading up to the final day (Tuesday) before the commencement of Lent on Ash Wednesday. **The day of Carnival, or Shrove Tuesday** is the climax of the pre-Lenten festivities. The name Carnival, of Italian derivation, means the *taking away of meat*, the *farewell to meat*; indicative of the fact the during the forty days of Lent, as anciently observed, the consumption of meat was disallowed. And, importantly, the Shrovetide itself echoes of an ancient period or periods devoted to atonement.

---

[12] John and Jesus symbolize the declining and rising phases of the sun, hence two suns at opposite polarities must be visualized so as to grasp their births opposite each other at the solstices, and Mission phases ending and beginning simultaneously at the equinoxes

Section One

The Secret Origins Of Judaism

Shrovetide or Shrove is derived from the word *shrive* which indicates an individual's *shriven* efforts toward forgiveness, reconciliation, penance, absolution, hence atonement. **As I indicated earlier in the essay**, rituals of atonement were commonly associated with the passing of the sun over the equinoxes, as the equinoxes signal the most dramatic shifts in the earthly environment; hence a pressing need, as perceived by primitive Man, for seeking atonement from the deities that he imagined governed the changing seasons.

You will find, that in many respects, the traditions of the vernal equinox and the autumnal equinox mirror each other. That the Jews seek atonement at the beginning of their civil year proximate to the *autumnal equinox*; while, on the other hand, the Christians seek atonement proximate the *vernal equinox* is indicative of a mirrored or quasi-mirrored reflection. **The Christian New Year, aforetime, commenced proximate to the vernal equinox** instead of January one as is now the case. Lent is seen as a period of preparation for Easter[13] by many Christians; **while amongst Jews the month of Elul**, which precedes Rosh Hashanah - the Jewish New Year, is viewed as a month of preparation for the Judaic New Year, and the Yom Kippur (Day of Atonement). **Both equinoxes** mark the back and forth movements of the sun between the hemispheres, therefore the symbolisms are often similar.

The Lent observance, itself, begins with Ash Wednesday which is signified by the mark of ashes, usually in the form of a cross, upon the foreheads of the faithful; ashes normally derived from the burning of palm branches or the burning of the grotesque effigy that signifies or personifies the Carnival. **The ashes are said to be a symbol of penance,** reflecting the eventual mortality of all - that we were created from dust (ashes) and to dust we shall return; *Job 42:6 Wherefore I abhor myself, and repent in dust and ashes.*

The period of Lent extends for forty days, from Ash Wednesday to Easter Sunday. **This period is actually** *forty-six days*, but since the six Sundays in

---

[13] Anciently Lent was seen as a preparation for the annual Baptisms of Easter as well

Section One

The Secret Origins Of Judaism

between Ash Wednesday and Easter are not included in the calculation, that reduces to forty days the actual Lent observances.

Nowadays, as previously indicated, the Lent season is seen as a time of penance, a time of self denial, a time of being shriven in imitation of the forty days temptation of Christ whereas, as the story goes, Christ was tried and tempted in the wilderness by Satan[14.] I find it totally illogical and nonsensical to believe that god (as Jesus is so called) could be tempted by the offering of worldly goods by Satan. Think of it - god who created and owns everything is tempted by Satan with the offer of worldly dominions. **After surviving the temptations,** his mission of salvation, *at age thirty*, was launched. **During the Lent season it was traditional that the faithful abstain** from the eating of meat and meat by-products such as cheese, eggs, milk, etc - the faithful also fasted at varying degrees of intensity.

All religious traditions have *spiritual* **and** *doctrinal* **significance** according to the Rabbis, Ministers, and Imams. **Our focus** is *not* on the religious explanations given by the clergy for the various traditions observed by the faithful; since we are convinced that the religious explanations and rationalizations came *after* the establishment of the various traditions and *not before* their enactments. **These cultural traditions, in many cases, were initially shaped and spawned in primordial times, long before the advent of our modern religions.**

We are interested in practical, real life, mundane explanations for the origins of religious rituals - that is to say the primal, primitive core or matrix upon which religious veneers were subsequently overlaid by the priesthood. **Our contention** is that all of our longstanding religious traditions, at their

---

[14] **Luke 4:2-7** Being forty days tempted of the devil. And in those days he did eat nothing: and when they were ended, he afterward hungered. And the devil said unto him, If thou be the Son of god, command this stone that it be made bread. And Jesus answered him, saying, It is written, That man shall not live by bread alone, but by every word of god. And the devil, taking him up into an high mountain, shewed unto him all the kingdoms of the world in a moment of time. And the devil said unto him, All this power will I give thee, and the glory of them: for that is delivered unto me; and to whomsoever I will I give it. If thou therefore wilt worship me, all shall be thine.

Section One

The Secret Origins Of Judaism

inceptions, were reflections of the *practical concerns* of the primordial tribes.

The religious and spiritual assertions that are sometimes used to rationalize our often bizarre cultural traditions are explanations engendered after the fact. The myths (make-do explanations) came about after the various rituals had become culturally habituated. We traditionally carry out religious rituals handed down to us by our forbears that we, in many cases, don't understand; in consequence we have created fanciful mythical tales as make-do explanations for these activities. The Jewish fairytale of Hebrew bondage in Egypt is a good example of *genuine* symbolic mythology, because this *bondage* symbolism actually symbolizes the bondage of the sun and the sun's emancipation when it passes over the vernal equinox; however, on the other hand, the mythical and juvenile explanations that the Jews give for their Passover rituals, such as the *salt water* of the Seder table setting representing the tears of their afflictions, are a prime example of *unfounded myth making* - that is to say deceptions and lies proffered to conceal the truth or to conceal their ignorance of the truth. The truth, of course, is defined as the *underlying physical reality* that the rituals symbolize. Myth and mythology is properly defined as allegory and symbolism, but some myths are simply lies or misrepresentations, designed to conceal the truth or, in some cases, to conceal ignorance of the true factors.

The underlying reality, which the Lent rituals quite evidently seem to symbolize, *pivot*, to an extent, around the 40-day[15] duration of the event, which has clear astro-theological implications; **but beyond that**, the forty days sequestration *is also* the **official definition** of *Quarantine*. Our ancestors were accustomed to quarantine ships at the dock for a period of forty days before allowing them to unload personnel or materials. This restriction was imposed to prevent the spread of contagion.

---

[15] As we have covered previously, oftentimes the 40-day span symbolizes seasonal transition within biblical mythology. The symbolism may point to either of the four cardinal points, though most often to the vernal or the autumnal equinox.

Section One

The Secret Origins Of Judaism

Also the fact that meat and meat by-products were disallowed during the forty days of Lent restrictions brings to mind that since the ancients were forced to endure the winter months in seclusion, and relied totally or almost totally on stowed provisions, mainly salted, dried, or smoked meats, cheeses, grains, and the like; **a major fear** that they faced during each winter's sojourn was *food contamination*. **A constant threat** was putrefaction of their meat stows; blight, bacterial or insect infestation of their grains and cheeses. These are the very items that were anciently disallowed during the Lent season. I have not uncovered a solid link in this regard in my research on the subject, but I feel the implications are intriguing. **There are indications** that the ancients may have been *accustomed to the forced disposal* of a portion of their stowed provisions that, as a matter of course, *became contaminated* before the expiration of the winter confinements.

It must also be remembered that the vaunted Spring Cleaning phenomena was a worldwide tradition in keeping with the applicable climatic exigencies of the various regions of our planet. It was policy throughout the regions of the world that experienced dramatic climatic changes during the winter, that the ancients *thoroughly clean* and *air out* their habitations at the end of the forced confinements of the winter months. These cleaning activities clearly smack of *hygienic renewal and sanitation concerns*. This phenomenon was not restricted to the Semites nor do I believe that the relevant symbolisms, in this regard, were restricted to the Semites. However, our *primary focus* shall, in the interest of clarity, remain with Judaic symbolisms and myths.

And it is important that we also remember that the spring cleaning tradition is in mighty force even to this day. It behooves us to think and reflect, and consider how important this ritual of *spring cleaning* must have been to overall sanitation, and to the health and vitality of our primitive ancestors of prehistory. They endured their winters without efficient heating systems, without running water, without toilet facilities, without changes of clothing, without windows, without reliable or consistent lighting. **Is it any wonder** that when spring finally sprung that they stripped themselves of their *filthy* and *infested* winter clothing, baptized or submerged their souls

Section One

The Secret Origins Of Judaism

into the local rivers, scraped the accumulated crud from their bodies, and *dawned new fresh clean garments* to bring in the new year, announced by the sun's passing over the vernal equinox at spring. **Please** *remember*, the ancient peasants did not possess, as a rule, changes of clothing - only what they wore on their persons. During the winter sequestration, they were *stuck* in these garments for the duration. **I think** that most of the spring rituals are logically understandable when we throw aside the spurious religious myths foisted by the clergy.

The Festival Of First Fruits

To recap *our objective* within this essay - we are reviewing the *Seven Jewish Feasts* pursuant to the invalidation of said Feasts as *integral to* and *evidence of* an alleged compact (Covenant) between god and the Jews. In the above, we have presented various biblical passages proffered by the Jews in support of their claim to divine patronage. **The Hebrews claim** that the Seven Jewish Feasts were mandated by god almighty himself as integral to the covenant between they and god. And accordingly, they have presented verses from the Torah (Bible) allegedly *in god's own words* that ostensibly lend support to this absurd assertion of a preferred status with god. **We, of course, view this claim as utter nonsense,** hence our goal, within this essay, is to link the Jewish festivals with their true pagan or primitive origins. The Festival of First Fruits or Bikkurim is the third observance of the Passover season.

To repeat, the Seven Jewish Feasts were all pre-existent, *in their basic forms*, *before* the advent of Judaism amongst the *Hebrew faction* of the ancient Semitic people. **These feasts** or festivals originated, in antiquity, as seasonal and agricultural festivals, prevalent among the Semitic tribes of the Middle East and the adjoining regions. **The rituals involved go back several generations,** or perhaps millennia I should say, as nature rites. **The festivals were originally designed** to mark and signal the changes of the seasons, and also the planting and harvesting of crops; and had no religious connection, at least not in the modern sense.

Section One

The Secret Origins Of Judaism

As the Hebrew priesthood commenced forming their religious doctrine, it behooved them to adopt some ingenious and actually peculiar methods by which the previously established traditions and ritualistic practices of their tribes could be integrated seamlessly, with a seemingly natural fit, into the newly evolving Judaic religion. **They clearly went over the top**, so to speak, in their attempts to apply a religious veneer to the Bikkurim festival i.e. Festival of First Fruits. See the biblical instruction for the faithful: *Leviticus 23:10-11 Speak unto the children of Israel, and say unto them, When ye be come into the land which I give unto you, and shall reap the harvest thereof, then ye shall bring a sheaf of the firstfruits of your harvest unto the priest: And he shall wave the sheaf before the LORD, to be accepted for you: on the morrow after the sabbath the priest shall wave it.*

Remember - allegedly this is god himself speaking in the bible; instructing the Hebrew faithful to wave the first fruits of the harvest before him (god) within the Temple. The *Feasts of First Fruits* is clearly an agricultural festival. It celebrates the first fruit of the harvest as the appellation (first fruits) indicates. **This feast, in its origination,** is plainly a *primitive agricultural festival* that has now been fitted, very awkwardly I might add, into Jewish religious doctrine.

The bringing of the first fruits to the priests to be waved before god clearly smacks of primitive superstitions. The presenting of the First Fruits to the priesthood, at the point when the crop was ripe and actually harvested, was clearly a tithing or similar levying mechanism whereby the tribal administration taxed the community. Before the evolution of organized modern religion amongst the Semites, the taxing procedure was probably rather straight forward - that all members of the tribe pay a portion (perhaps 1/10th) of their crop to the governing (tribal) authority. Of course, in some cases, the primitives sought the blessings of their deities on their plantings or harvest through various supplicatory rituals. **Ancient primitives from all the corners of the world have practiced many strange, bizarre rituals, born out of ignorance and superstition,** according to our historians, anthropologists, and archeologists; **but** of *this* ritual i.e. waving the sheaf, **we are told by the Jews** that this waving of the

Section One

The Secret Origins Of Judaism

Sheaf was commanded by god almighty. **In their attempt** to make this stipulation a godly command, the Rabbis have produced a really weird sounding spectacle, in my opinion - picture the priests inside the Temple waving a crop offering back and forth before god in the hope that god will bless the crops. This action is done by god's command according to the bible! I find it incomprehensible, as well as irrational to believe that god almighty has demanded that these rituals be performed in perpetuity as part of a godly covenant; and the consequent incredulity of this Jewish assertion gives further support of our counter-assertion that the Judaic claim of a godly covenant is fraudulent, from beginning to end.

The question that lurches us into a quandary, perplexed and befuddled is this: if we admit within ourselves that this claim and other similar Jewish claims of the bible cannot be literally true, then what course of action is demanded of us as believers and followers of monotheistic doctrines. Should our faith remain undiminished? Shall we give the various biblical inconsistencies a pass? **Shall we pick and choose** from amongst the bible edicts *those* that we judge as congruous and veritable, and just disregard or overlook the more troubling aspects - and yet remain assured within our heart of hearts that we are on the correct path to god or salvation; or will we *muster the courage* to subject our *inherited beliefs* to a serious reevaluation?

Shavuot, Feast Of Weeks

The gist of our premise is that the bible is not literally true, but rather is a book of mythology, symbolisms, and allegories. **We assert** that at the core of all genuine mythologies there lies an *underlying physical or cultural reality* that the mythological symbolisms, in fact, represent. **Also**, the Judaic or Israelite tales narrated in the bible are not historical, but rather *mythological stories* with underlying real world interpretations. **Our goal** is to connect the biblical mythologies with their true *inner or underlying* meanings. **We further assert** that the biblical New Testament is, in many respects, a revised copy of the Old Testament; that when the *Jewish* authors composed the New Testament, they used the Old Testament as *source material* for the fictional stories that make up the New Testament. **Our task**

Section One

The Secret Origins Of Judaism

also, is to expose the linkages between the Old and New Testaments that prove that the New has been copied, with revisions, from the Old. This, we shall do as our series continues.

It is important that we remember that *scientific mythology* is a symbolic language that *shields* an *underlying reality*, so that the true or accurate interpretations can only be obtained by those who are conversant with the esoteric symbolisms (codes); **likewise** with *environmental mythology*, which we have subjected to significant scrutiny thus far in our essay, it too, though easier to decipher, cannot be properly decoded without some esoteric insights and familiarity with the particular culture under focus.

Scientific and Environmental mythology have evolved from ancient times to the present; that is to say, our understanding of natural and supernatural phenomena has evolved and the methodologies by which we encode our research data and decipher the research data of prior generations is evolving in step with the unfolding ages, as we recover from the Dark Ages of some past generations. **This evolution will continue**, partly through systems of exposition and exegesis of the ancient allegorical data, as more and more bright and enlightened minds evaluate the ancient scriptures, over time - so as extrapolate greater and greater truths from the storehouses of data discovered and preserved by the ancients within the vast multicultural mythological matrix at our disposal, and subject to our review.

However we must be circumspect, because some mythologies have been insidiously manipulated by the priesthood so as to divert the common minds away from the underlying truths, not just to shield the codes (that define the underlying realities) from contamination, but also, with pernicious and predacious intent, to deceive and mislead the masses; and to create false impressions. **Such is the case with much of the Judaic symbolism** - the Rabbis have invented a mythical Jewish history through the use of their concocted biblical scriptures. The *exact* true history of the *original Semitic* Jewish people, nurtured by the ancient Sumerians and others, is not *fully* known. We can piece together their probable history by comparisons with other ancient Semitic tribes and cultures; but that is not our goal within this

Section One

The Secret Origins Of Judaism

book. **We are focused** on unveiling the underlying realities that the scriptural and other symbolisms have obscured from our intellectual sights.

Parallels of the Omer to the Hebrews

The Shavuot harvest is the conclusion of the Grain Harvesting that began with the *Barley Harvest* of Bikkurim fifty days earlier with the waving of the Omer in the Temple on the day after the Sabbath; however Sabbath may be defined, whether as a *Saturday* Sabbath or a *Holiday* Sabbath. **Shavuot marks the reaping** of the *Wheat Harvest*, undertaken seven weeks after the commencement of the Barley Harvest during the Passover season.

The Hebrews are said, according to the bible, to have exited Egypt concurrent with the offering or waving of the Omer (sheaf) in the Temple. **The waving of the sheaf** offering was done on the *day after* (morrow after) Passover, and **likewise** the bible asserts that **the Hebrews exited Egypt** on the *day after* the Passover. We arrive at the festival of Shavuot (Feast of Weeks) after the passing of seven weeks. **The festival of Shavuot** is celebrated with a Bread Offering, that is, <u>two loaves of bread</u> are baked from the new wheat harvest and waved before Yahweh. **This corresponds** to the Israelites arriving at **Mount Sinai,** at Shavuot, and the dispensation of the Ten Commandments on <u>two stone tablets</u>. --- *Numbers 33:3 And they departed from Rameses in the first month, on the fifteenth day of the first month;* <u>*on the morrow after the passover the children of Israel went out*</u> *with an high hand in the sight of all the Egyptians.* --- **When the Passover is marked as a Sabbath**, which is the standard custom among Jews, the symbolism or correspondence of the *Omer* and of *Israel* are kept in sync, with both events taking place the day after the Sabbath - note: *Leviticus 23:11 And he shall wave the sheaf before the LORD, to be accepted for you:* <u>*on the morrow after the sabbath*</u> *the priest shall wave it.*

At the Shavuot feast two loaves of bread were prepared from the new harvest as an offering to Yahweh, (Leviticus 23:17 Ye shall bring out of your habitations <u>two wave loaves</u> of two tenth deals: they shall be of fine flour; they shall be baken with leaven; they are the firstfruits unto the LORD) **and consequently**

Section One

The Secret Origins Of Judaism

the parallels are closely maintained by the reciprocal offering, we might say, of two stone tablets upon which the Ten Commandments have been engraved. (Exodus 31:18 And he gave unto Moses, when he had made an end of communing with him upon mount Sinai, two tables of testimony, tables of stone, written with the finger of god). The Hebrews exited Egypt on the morrow after the Passover which corresponds exactly to the Omer offering in the Temple. Fifty days later Moses received the Ten Commandments from Yahweh engraved on Two Stone Tablets, on Mount Sinai - this corresponds exactly to the offering of Two Loaves of bread in the Temple before the Hebrew Deity.

My point is this: we know that the agricultural traditions *preceded* the Judaic tale of the Israeli exodus from Egypt - that the Exodus never really occurred; **moreover, it is clear** from the biblical rendering of the Egyptian-Israel saga that the Rabbis purposely composed the exodus or movements of the *fictional* Israel to match the movements, so to speak, of the Omer. The offering of the Omer before god in the Temple corresponds to the Israeli Exodus, and the seven week counting from the wave offering to the Wheat Harvest fifty days later corresponds to the arrival of the Hebrews at Mt. Sinai fifty days later. It's easy to see the workings of the *Rabbinic mind* as they purposely **composed their mythos so as to match** the prevailing **rituals** that were already in place among the agrarian Semites.

Please indulge me as I digress briefly - concerning the biblical exodus of the Israelites from Egypt. According to the bible, a minimum of six hundred thousand (600,000) people were involved in this exodus. I say minimum, because the count, according to the bible, was restricted to those who were *twenty years of age or older*. Mind you, this massive amount of people were allegedly contacted and organized, and subsequently debarked from Egypt *in one day* without prior notice, at the whim of Pharaoh. And need I remind you, they did not possess modern electronic means of communication as we do, nor modern means of loading and hauling their cargo. The exodus occurred on the same day that Pharaoh ordered their departure. Talk about a logistical nightmare! And they departed with no particular destination, just three days journey into the desert according to the bible - they ended up

Section One

The Secret Origins Of Judaism

spending *forty years* in the desert and eating manna daily dropped from the skies by Yahweh.... *Exodus 16:35 And the children of Israel did eat manna forty years, until they came to a land inhabited; they did eat manna, until they came unto the borders of the land of Canaan....*This yarn is so absurd and unbelievable, it makes me wonder how we ever fell into the belief of such nonsense! *Numbers 1:45-46 So were all those that were numbered of the children of Israel, by the house of their fathers, from twenty years old and upward, all that were able to go forth to war in Israel; Even all they that were numbered were six hundred thousand and three thousand and five hundred and fifty....* So the monotheists assert unabashedly that this absurdity actually took place as proclaimed within the bible, that nearly a million people, if not more (when considering those under the age of twenty who were not counted) plus animals, livestock etc were organized in less than a day, and a headcount made no less - and wandered in the desert for forty years, surviving on bread dropped daily from the sky!

Parallels of Shavuot and Pentecost

Shavuot commemorates the dispensation of the Torah to Moses on Mt Sinai. This same date is the Pentecost of the Christians. The symbolisms pertaining to the *Jewish Shavuot* (Feast of Weeks), and the *Christian Pentecost*, are clear examples of fictional religious veneers being painted over an underlying agricultural festival that, in its origination, had no religious significance whatsoever.

The Christian symbolism shows Jesus as the first sheaf or Firstfruit (Omer) offered or sacrificed to god as a propitiatory payment: *(Leviticus 23:10-11 Speak unto the children of Israel, and say unto them, When ye be come into the land which I give unto you, and shall reap the harvest thereof, then ye shall bring a sheaf of the firstfruits of your harvest unto the priest: And he shall wave the sheaf before the LORD, to be accepted for you: on the morrow after the sabbath the priest shall wave it.)* He, the mythical Jesus was cut from life, as a copy of the sheaf that was cut from the earth, bundled and offered (waved before Lord) to god in the Temple as the First Fruit of the harvest on the Sunday morning after the Saturday Sabbath.... *1Corinthians 15:20 But now is Christ risen from the dead, and become the firstfruits of them that slept.*

Section One

The Secret Origins Of Judaism

In the Christian mystic symbolism, the cutting apart or slaying of Jesus, and his resurrection unto the Father god on the morrow (Sunday) after the Sabbath, following his crucifixion, is an allegorical or *crafted mythical copy of the Jewish tradition* of cutting and offering the Firstfruit to the Lord within the Temple on the morrow after the *Saturday* Sabbath that follows the Passover feast. **Then fifty days later, at the festival of Shavuot,** when the second *Jewish* offering (two loaves of Bread) of the *wheat* harvest is made, the Holy Spirit is said to have descended upon the disciples at the Christian Pentecost (Jewish Shavuot) in dispensation i.e. Speaking in Tongues - this Christian tradition (Pentecost) is in exact duplication of the Jewish tradition wherein the Torah was dispensed by god to Moses on Mt. Sinai. **The Old Testament states** that god descended amongst thunder and lightening to Mt. Sinai and dispensed unto the Israelites the Ten Commandments, carved in stone. **The New Testament states** that on the *same date* the spirit of god descended on the gathered apostles amidst thunder, wind, and fire and spoke in tongues to the assembled. Clearly, the new has been copied from the old.

Note the biblical reference to the two sacrificial Sheaf offerings separated by an interval of seven weeks or fifty days: .... *Leviticus 23:15-16 And ye shall count unto you from the morrow after the sabbath, from the day that ye brought the sheaf of the wave offering; seven sabbaths shall be complete: Even unto the morrow after the seventh sabbath shall ye number fifty days; and ye shall offer a new meat offering unto the LORD.*

Now Compare the two episodes of the Shavuot festival, that is to say, *the dispensation of the Law* (Torah, Ten Commandments) to Moses and *the dispensation by the Holy Spirit* to the Disciples, and see clearly how the new style Jews i.e. Christian-Jews have, by way of the Pentecostal story, simply created a fictional Christian replication to their Jewish Shavuot tradition, which is likewise established on a *fabricated* premise. *Acts 2:1-4 And when the day of Pentecost was fully come, they were all with one accord in one place. And suddenly there came a sound from heaven as of a rushing mighty wind, and it filled all the house where they were sitting. And there appeared unto them cloven tongues like as of fire, and it sat upon each of them. And they were all filled with the*

Section One

The Secret Origins Of Judaism

Holy Ghost, and began to speak with other tongues, as the Spirit gave them utterance.

Now compare this Christian Pentecostal dispensation, in the above, to the prior Jewish dispensation, at the Shavuot feast, made to Moses and the Children of Israel at Mount Sinai: *Exodus 19:16-20 And it came to pass on the third day in the morning, that there were <u>thunders and lightnings</u>, and a thick cloud upon the mount, and the voice of the trumpet exceeding loud; so that all the people that was in the camp trembled. And Moses brought forth the people out of the camp to meet with god; and they stood at the nether part of the mount. And mount Sinai was altogether on a smoke, because the <u>LORD descended upon it in fire</u>: and the smoke thereof ascended as the smoke of a furnace, and the whole mount quaked greatly. And when the voice of the trumpet sounded long, and waxed louder and louder, Moses spake, and god answered him by a voice. And the LORD came down upon mount Sinai, on the top of the mount: and the LORD called Moses up to the top of the mount; and Moses went up.*

We see that in the Old Testament, god is depicted as descending amongst *smoke and fire and thunder* to speak with Moses and those assembled with him on the occasion of the *Feast Of Weeks* i.e. Shavuot; and lo and behold, in the New Testament, at an annual recurrence of the same festival, that is to say, Shavuot, called Pentecost by the Christians, the Holy Spirit descended amongst *thunderous sounds from heaven, mighty winds, and tongues of fire,* no less; that spoke in a cacophony of diverse languages to the Disciples and those assembled with them.

Of course, both the Jewish and Christian renditions of these alleged communications with god almighty are completely absurd, ludicrous, and irrational when taken literally. It is palpably clear, from the parallels of the context in both yarns, that the Christian-Jews that authored the New Testament version *used their Old Testament texts as a guide* in formulating this new Christian rendition of an old Jewish farcical tale. **The most important factor** that we need to remember or retain is that both tales, Jewish and Christian, have been layered upon an ancient pagan agricultural festival (Shavuot, Feast of Weeks) that has no genuine religious connection whatsoever.

Section One

The Secret Origins Of Judaism

It is well known among the researchers of religious origins, that the policy of *cultural adaptation* was universally used by the various religious clergies as they sought to evolve the ancient primitives into higher forms (more sophisticated forms) of religion. The clergies of those ancient times (when respectively, Judaism, Christianity, and lastly Islam were in their infancies) were not able to dislodge the various peoples from their old pagan customs, so they allowed the populace to keep their longstanding culturally ingrained customs; *but the old primitive customs were painted over with a new religious veneer*, that gave new updated religious explanations for the varied primitive customs or traditions. So nowadays the faithful among the monotheists show great reverence to various current religious traditions, that in truth, are little more than repackaged forms of ancient pagan ceremonies.

Insights into the Traditions of Shavuot

The Feast Of Weeks is the fourth of the seven Jewish feasts, called *Shavuot* by the Jews. This festival, which is ordained by god according to the bible, comes fifty days after the Bikkurim festival, that is to say, fifty days after the waving of the *First Fruits* before god in the Jewish Temple. *Leviticus 23:15-17 And ye shall count unto you from the morrow after the sabbath, from the day that ye brought the sheaf of the wave offering; seven sabbaths shall be complete: Even unto the morrow after the seventh sabbath shall ye number fifty days; and ye shall offer a new meat offering unto the LORD. Ye shall bring out of your habitations two wave loaves of two tenth deals: they shall be of fine flour; they shall be baken with leaven; they are the firstfruits unto the LORD.*

Traditionally, the Jews see the festival of Shavuot as the event which marks their spiritual redemption, and the confirmation of the Covenant between they and god by the blessed *gift of the Torah*, which they claim occurred during the time of this festival at Mount Sinai. The Torah is the helpmate (Bride) of the Jewish people bestowed by god to his chosen, according to Judaic doctrine. In another phase of Judaic tradition, the Jewish people view themselves *as god's Temple*, in which god dwells and works his (God's) will. They fashion themselves as the Bride and Yahweh as the Bridegroom. This symbolism is, of course, paralleled amongst the Christians who claim

Section One

The Secret Origins Of Judaism

that the Christian Church is the Bride of Jesus the Bridegroom. The Torah and the event of its dispensation at Mt. Sinai (symbolically the mount of the moon-god <u>Sin</u>-ai), in effect, solemnifies the covenant (marriage contract) between god and the Jews.

In the Jewish view, their physical liberation was accomplished during Passover when god freed them, that is, according to their mythological doctrine, from bondage to Egypt. Subsequently, in turn, their *Spiritual* liberation and official manumission was sealed at Shavuot by reason of the *visitation of god* at Mount Sinai and the gift of the Torah, which in effect, certified the compact or covenant between they and God. This event took place fifty days after the exodus from Egypt, in sync with the seven week or fifty day count down (Counting of the Omer) from the Bikkurim or First Fruits *waving*[16] ritual of the Passover season.

The fifty-day interval between the waving of the *barley sheaf* in the Temple at Bikkurim and the *wheat offering* of Shavuot is called the *Counting of the Omer*. The Omer refers to the measure of the Sheaf (First Fruits) offered at Bikkurim. The interval of fifty days is considered a time of mourning and reflection; I assume similar in tone to Lent. The process of barley harvesting commenced with Bikkurim, right after Passover day, and **the process of wheat harvesting commences** with the *Feast of Weeks* or *Shavuot*, after a count-down of fifty days from Bikkurim. The bible instructs that at the time of Shavuot, the Jews must bake two loaves of bread from the wheat harvest, and ritualistically offer these loaves to god within the Temple.

The ceremonies of Shavuot includes various religious readings or recitals. The reading of the Torah is paramount, with emphasis on the gift of the Torah to the Jews at Mount Sinai, inclusive of the popular *Ten Commandments* of course. **Diligent study and reflection** in the Torah is observed - it is traditional to stay awake all night *in dedicated study of the*

---

[16] That is the waving of the Sheaf of Firstfruits in the Temple

Section One

The Secret Origins Of Judaism

Torah on the first day of the festival. **The Jews decorate their dwellings and Synagogues with greenery and flowers** in commemoration of the festival. The Shavuot menus always include dairy products and also baked bread, as well as several other choices of vegetables..................
I must interject at this point that one *cannot* achieve a full grasp of Judaic traditions from the reading of the bible or the Torah *only* - more information is needed than that supplied within the unamplified bible. Much of the biblical scripture revolves around the *Temple Cult* form of Judaism, that is to say, the incessant blood letting; the daily ritualistic slaughtering of animals upon alters, the sprinkling of the animals blood about the environs, incense burning, and all such strange, bizarre goings on - these primitive activities are not conducted by modern Jews, to the best of my knowledge.

The Jewish priesthood i.e. Rabbis, centuries ago, came up with an *ingenious system* by which they could evolve, edit, and adapt their belief system in keeping with the exigencies of evolving Jewish culture, onward into the indefinite future. **The Rabbis instituted a system** by which their scriptures are a *Living* scripture, *not locked in time*, but culturally adaptive by way of tactical *exegetical reinterpretations and addendums* to the scriptures. **They, the Rabbis, claimed** that when god revealed the Torah, he actually revealed *two Torahs* in tandem, one *written* and the other *Oral*. The Oral Torah was disseminated verbally by Moses to a select group that maintained the Oral Torah over the generations. **Therefore** the Rabbis were able to use or *expound the Oral Torah, by the spoken tongue*, so as to enhance the understanding and utilization of the *Written Torah*. The Priests have cunningly edited their bible so as to support their claim of the dual Torah, one *Written* and dispensed to Moses only and the other *Oral*, and dispensed to the priesthood i.e. the Rabbis, as well as to Moses. See bible.......*Numbers 11:16-17 And the LORD said unto Moses, Gather unto me seventy men [Sanhedrin]of the elders of Israel, whom thou knowest to be the elders of the people, and officers over them; and bring them unto the tabernacle of the congregation, that they may stand there with thee. And I will come down and talk with thee there: and I will take of the spirit which is upon thee, and will put it upon them; and they shall bear the burden of the people with thee, that thou bear it not thyself alone*

Section One

The Secret Origins Of Judaism

Several hundred years ago, circa the 3rd Century A.D., the Rabbis decided to put portions of the Oral Torah into writing as a more convenient and effective way of circulating and preserving the Oral Torah. **The written form of the *Oral Torah* is called *Mishnah*, and is contained within the *Talmud*.** Another major section of the Talmud is called *Gemara* - **the Gemara is** a compilation of extensive commentaries made by various Rabbis, over the centuries, on the meanings of the Mishnah (Oral Torah). The Talmud was compiled or completed, according to most reports, by the 6th century A.D., both the *Jerusalem Talmud*, and the *Babylonian Talmud*. **As an additional religious reference**, the Jews also have the **Midrash** or *Midrashim* in plural. The Midrashim contain commentaries or exegesis on the *written* Jewish bible inclusive of the *Written Torah*. **So it follows,** that in order to achieve a full and comprehensive picture of Jewish Traditions, we must expand our search beyond the bible per se and include the various other references penned by the Rabbis and Jewish sages. **Actually**, when we expand our search into the ancillary religious commentaries, we may encounter differences of opinions from various Jewish factions such as the **Pharisees, Sadducees,** the **Samaritans**, and others.

It's abundantly clear from our research, and the research of others, that the Judaic religion underwent extensive revision between perhaps the 4th century B.C., on into the early centuries of the Common Era, and continued to adapt itself under influential Rabbis; so that modern Judaism is most accurately described as Rabbinic Judaism. The traditions of *biblical Judaism* have been shelved to a significant degree by the Rabbis, and a detailed *truthful* account of the Judaism practiced before the advent of the Common Era has been obscured from view and otherwise misrepresented. **Judaic history as related in the bible is very unreliable** because the tales of the bible are thoroughly interwoven with myths. **The tales** of a great Judaic kingdom, existent prior to the Common Era, with a marvelous Temple at Jerusalem are not confirmed in secular history. **In fact King David**, Solomon, and other alleged Israelites notables, as well as the alleged Jerusalem Temple, as described in the bible, cannot be found in secular

Section One

The Secret Origins Of Judaism

history. More details *and vivid proofs* on this will be unveiled as our series of essays progresses.

Notes on Shavuot Traditions

According to Jewish tradition, the Feast of Weeks (Shavuot) commemorates the revelation of the Torah to Moses on Mount Sinai. The bible states that at the time of Shavuot, in the Sinai desert, at Mount Sinai, god appeared to Moses, with great clamor and flare, that is to say thunder and lightning and such, and sealed his covenant with the Jewish people. **Moses went up to the heights of the mountain, as the story goes, and the Israelites stood apart below**, but in sight and hearing of this miraculous spectacle, as god almighty held conference with Moses. The Jews tell us that during this momentous event god wrote from his own hand or whatever the *Ten Commandments* upon two carved stone tablets. Witness the following bible verses that describe the event: --- *Exodus 19:1 In the third month, when the children of Israel were gone forth out of the land of Egypt, the same day came they into the wilderness of Sinai... Exodus 19:3-5 And Moses went up unto god, and the LORD called unto him out of the mountain, saying, Thus shalt thou say to the house of Jacob, and tell the children of Israel; Ye have seen what I did unto the Egyptians, and how I bare you on eagles' wings, and brought you unto myself. Now therefore, if ye will obey my voice indeed, and keep my covenant, then ye shall be a peculiar treasure unto me above all people: for all the earth is mine:... Exodus 19:9 And the LORD said unto Moses, Lo, I come unto thee in a thick cloud, that the people may hear when I speak with thee, and believe thee for ever. And Moses told the words of the people unto the LORD.... Exodus 19:16 And it came to pass on the third day in the morning, that there were thunders and lightnings, and a thick cloud upon the mount, and the voice of the trumpet exceeding loud; so that all the people that was in the camp trembled.... Exodus 19:18 **And mount Sinai was altogether on a smoke**, because the LORD descended upon it in fire: and the smoke thereof ascended as the smoke of a furnace, and the whole mount quaked greatly.... Exodus 19:20 **And the LORD came down upon mount Sinai**, on the top of the mount: and the LORD called Moses up to the top of the mount; and Moses went up.*

The first major appearance of god to Moses was from the midst of a Burning Bush, a bush that burned but however was not consumed by the

Section One

The Secret Origins Of Judaism

flames. *Exodus 3:2-4 And the angel of the LORD appeared unto him in a flame of fire out of the midst of a bush: and he looked, and, behold, the bush burned with fire, and the bush was not consumed. And Moses said, I will now turn aside, and see this great sight, why the bush is not burnt. And when the LORD saw that he turned aside to see, god called unto him out of the midst of the bush, and said, Moses, Moses. And he said, Here am I.*

The second major appearance of god to Moses, noted above from the 19th chapter of Exodus, was much more awe inspiring, when you consider the thunder, lightening, smoke, quaking, and all the rest. I think that the second editor had a much more vivid *imagination* than the first. **I find it somewhat perplexing** that there are some, or I should say, actually many people who sincerely believe that this story is the accounting of an actual historical event - such irrationality, i.e. the acceptance of biblical stories that are *palpable fairytales* as factual, is astounding to those of us who are realistic, rational beings.

This festival is a very clear example of how the Judaic priesthood has constructed the Jewish religion around pre-existent pagan festivals. Of the seven Jewish feasts, Shavuot (The Feast of Weeks) is the only feast that sets more or less to itself in the calendar. The Feast of Weeks is clearly a festival derived from ancient pagan agricultural rites that, as the rituals of the feast clearly indicate, celebrated the closing of the grain harvesting. That the Jews have converted or merged this ancient pre-Judaic perennial harvest ceremony into a modern religious tradition cannot be rationally doubted.

Shavuot is observed in the third month of the Hebrew calendar, most notably on Sivan 6; it comes about seven weeks after the Passover festivals and about sixteen weeks before Rosh Hashanah, the Jewish *Lunar* New year. **The other six** of the seven major Jewish feasts are clustered about the equinoxes. The equinoxes, both the *vernal* and the *autumnal* mark the passages of the sun between the upper and lower cosmic hemispheres. Passover (Pesach), The Feast of Unleavened Bread (Hag Hamatzah), and The Festival of the Firstfruits (Bikkurim) are all proximate to the Vernal Equinox; while the Jewish Lunar New Year (Rosh Hashanah), Day of

Section One

The Secret Origins Of Judaism

Atonement (Yom Kippur), and Tabernacles (Sukkoth) are clustered about the Autumnal Equinox.

The equinoctial Festivals and their symbolisms, both *vernal* and *autumnal*, are very similar at multiple levels of interpretation. The equinoctial festivals, which are geared to tracking the movements of the sun between the hemispheres, go further back in history or prehistory (prehistory indicates before the establishment of written records or decipherable depictions) than the **agricultural festivals**, which signal planting and harvesting. I cover this aspect, somewhat, in my book *Lifting the Gnostic Veil* under the explanations of the Noah mythology. The Noachian symbolisms reflect, in some respects, an earlier form of the Hebrew calendar. **As I noted above, the present Jewish festivals reflect the blending** of two Semitic cultures into one, that is to say, the merging of the nomads (shepherds) and the farmers under one central authority.

Of the seven Jewish festivals, three are described as *Ingathering* festivals, which simply means appointed times to *gather in* the crops - in other words a time appointed to harvest crops. **The three harvest feasts** are Pesach (Passover), Shavuot (Feast of Weeks), and Sukkoth (Tabernacles). **Harvesting, in ancient times, was a community effort**, whereas the entire farming community, more or less, focused on the harvesting, processing, and stowing of the crops. **The harvesting and processing of the resultant foodstuffs had to be accomplished within certain limits of time** as dictated by the weather, the ripeness of the crops and the viability of the crops going forward; for example, if the rains arrived before the grains were sufficiently harvested, processed, and stowed, much would be lost due to rot. **The ancient Hebrews planted a variety** of grains such as wheat, barley, rye and other crops. They also cultivated figs, pomegranates, dates, olives, grapes, and perhaps various other crops. These crops were planted and harvested at varying times of the year depending on the nature of the particular crop.

Section One

The Secret Origins Of Judaism

Rosh Hashanah

From this point, we shall review the **Fall Festivals** of *Rosh Hashanah, Yom Kippur*, and *Sukkoth*. We shall insert biblical verses pertinent to these festivals (feasts), along with our inputs on Judaic and other traditions. **We shall offer** our commentaries, analyzations, and some additional insights. Quite frankly, the biblical verses themselves are clear testimonies to the pagan origins of the Judaic Feasts and Sabbaths. **Our goal** is to invalidate the false assertion of the Hebrews that their Religious Festivals have been ordained by god. **To a great extant**, this invalidation is accomplished simply by exposing the absurdities of the biblically invoked Judaic rituals to the light of day. We shall highlight the similarities of biblically endorsed Jewish rituals to the pagan rites of other primal societies. We shall include important commentaries on the Judaic calendar.

Rosh Hashanah means *head of the year* - it is the Jewish New Year. Rosh Hashanah, which falls on the first day of the seventh (Jewish) month of Tishri, is the fifth of the seven major Jewish festivals - it is followed by Yom Kippur (Day of Atonement) on the tenth of Tishri, and then Sukkoth (Tabernacles) which commences on the fifteenth of Tishri. All three of these festivals are proximate to the *autumnal equinox*, the cosmic juncture at which the sun descends into the lower hemisphere.

It is significant that the Jews celebrate their New Year in the seventh month rather than in the first month of their year. **The Jewish year actually begins on Nisan one**, according to biblical directives. According to the bible, the Hebrews departed from Egypt in the month of Nisan (Abib), and the bible states that the month (Nisan) of the exodus should mark the beginnings of the Jewish years - *Exodus 12:2 This month shall be unto you the beginning of months: it shall be the first month of the year to you.* **However the Jews**, under Rabbinic direction, have chosen to mark their New Years at the *descent* of the sun (autumnal equinox) rather than at the *ascent* of the sun (vernal equinox).

Jewish days, months, and years always begin in the evening under darkness or at the approach of darkness. This is so because they measure

Section One

The Secret Origins Of Judaism

their days and months by the sightings of the moon, and since the moon is more easily seen under dark or dimmed skies, they therefore commence their days in the evening. **The first day of any month is called Rosh Chodesh** i.e. the head of the month, the **New Moon**. Six (6) PM, mathematically, marks the start of the evening, hence the start of the Jewish day and month. **Anciently**, strict tradition called for the month to begin *only at the actual sighting* of the New Moon, which (sighting) must be confirmed by at least *two witnesses*, and later certified by the **Sanhedrin** - an assembly of Jewish clerics with authority over such matters. So, of course, it is not unusual for the actual observed sighting of the New Moon to occur outside of the mathematical calculations that set the start of the Jewish day at six o'clock in the evening.

Nowadays, most Jews use a religious calendar that notes the dates of all the New Moons throughout the year, thereby making the actual viewing of the New Moon and the subsequent required corroboration of this viewing by, at least, two witnesses unnecessary.

We need to keep in mind, as our essay progresses, that originally, in the early years of Judaic culture, that **the beginnings of their months were not determined** *in advance* by dates on their calendars, but rather by the *actual physical sightings* of the New Moons throughout the year. **The method of counting** *day one* of each month from the sighting of the New Moon was obligatory in keeping with Judaic religious doctrine. Jewish cultural life is charted by the Judaic calendar, and it follows that the use of this unique calendar is indispensable to the protocols of the Jewish religion. **The Jewish people are required,** by godly decree according to the bible, to observe several rituals throughout the year *at appointed times*. **The Judaic calendar** is like a *sacred religious guide* that maps the required religious functions of the Jewish people throughout the year. The Jewish calendar, by design, is a religious (ecclesiastical) calendar, not a civil calendar.

Under modern Rabbinic Judaism the Jews use a *calculated* calendar, a reformed calendar, wherein the *festival dates* are preset within the yearly calendar. This calendar was adopted centuries ago for practical reasons. **The**

Section One

The Secret Origins Of Judaism

calendar uses a **Metonic system of calculation** whereas the Jewish lunar months are kept in sync with the seasons of the year, by utilizing seven Leap years in a 19 year lunar/solar cycle. We will review the Metonic cycle shortly.

Evidence indicates that the Metonic system of calculating the calendar was not consistent amongst the Hebrews before well into the Common Era. The Metonic calendar calculates when the *New Moon* is scheduled to appear, and notes such dates in advance on the calendar. **However**, the Judaic *biblical calendar* evolved from month to month as the cycles of the moon unfolded - the first day of the month was not known until it appeared *signaled* by the New Moon. The calculations of the Metonic calendar are very good, but not exact, because the calculations are based on averages. The calendar is very important because the calendar tracks the seasons and dictates when traditional activities and the festivals are to be observed.

These activities involved *methods of observing* the cosmic lights so as to measure the seasons. The planting and harvesting, ranching, slaughtering and butchering, weaving and sewing, building, preserving and stowing of food stuffs were all undertaken in relationship to the comings and goings of the seasons as they were noted in their calendars, or expected based on past experiences. The Hebrews got their cues for conducting these civil activities, in those formative years, by tracking the lunar cycles and by actual observations of the stars, and sun as indicators. So transferring from this system of observation, which was tested and true, to a calendar with calculated dates for the festivals or *appointed times* was a major adjustment. Also the move to calculation does not conform with the biblical directives which stipulate that the months must be measured by actual visual observations.

Section One

The Secret Origins Of Judaism

Again, it is to be noted, Rosh Hashanah is the *lunar* New Years[17] day, as stipulated or ordained by the Rabbis; although the *bible* sets *Nisan one* as the beginning of the Jewish year. The Jewish day starts in the evening at sunset, or mathematically at 6 PM. **As to symbolic or mythological parallels**, the *setting of the sun*, in the *24-hour daily cycle*; and in likeness, *the descent of the sun* annually *below the equinoxes into the underworld*, are both paralleled in their symbolisms. **In other words**, the autumnal equinox and 6:PM are parallel symbols - when the sun falls below the **autumnal equinox** it goes into winter darkness in the *annual cycle*; and theoretically if the day and night are equal, when the sun tracks pass **6:PM** it falls into the darkness or night of the *24-hour cycle*.

The *autumnal equinox* of the *annual* cycle correlates to the *sunset* of the *daily* cycle in the symbolisms, hence *the starting of the Jewish year* as the sun falls below the autumnal equinox and *the starting of the Jewish day* as the sun falls below the western horizon are mythological parallels. I am sure that this, the synchronization of the *evening of the year* with the *evening of the day*, was the major reason, among other reasons, that the *Rabbis overruled the biblical editors*, and put the *New Year designation* at Tishri rather than at Nisan as called for by the *Judaic god* of the bible; or more correctly, the *Jewish scribes* masquerading as god. **The Jewish scribes impudently wrote the bible, with unmatched gall and unbridled irreverence** for the true Unknown god, under the absurd *pretence* of actually being god or prophets of god.

The biblical stipulations as regards Tishri One are as follows: Leviticus 23:24-25 Speak unto the children of Israel, saying, In the seventh month, in the first day of the month, shall ye have a sabbath, a memorial of blowing of

---

[17] The lunar year is about 354 days, whilst the solar year is about 365 days. The year marked in the Autumn by Rosh Hashanah (New Years Day) is not a complete 365 day year - except in those leap years when the Jewish lunar calendar is brought into sync with the solar year by the insertion of an additional month i.e. Adar 2, in the Spring.

Section One

The Secret Origins Of Judaism

trumpets, an holy convocation. Ye shall do no servile work therein: but ye shall offer an offering made by fire unto the LORD. The primary directive given by the biblical editors for Tishri 1 is that it be a Sabbath, and that the festival reoccur annually, be memorialized as it were. **As regards its actual functionality within the calendar, Sabbath simply means to** pause, rest, pivot, commence, or not count (blank calendar date, epagomenal) in its operative context, **although religiously** the Sabbaths were days of spiritual devotion, and dedication or exclusive service to god.

The <u>correlations</u> of the *annual* cycle to the *daily* cycle in terms of *symbolic parallels* **are designated by the <u>cardinal points</u> to <u>clock time</u>**, which therefore denotes the *Vernal Equinox to Sunrise, Summer Solstice to High Noon, Autumnal Equinox to Sunset*, and the *Winter Solstice to Midnight*. **So starting the year** at the autumnal equinox <u>corresponds</u> to **starting the day** at 6 PM at night in terms of parallel symbolisms. Rosh Hashanah marks the autumnal equinox, and the autumnal equinox is equivalent to six o'clock in the evening or the beginning of darkness in the symbolism[18].

As noted above, the reason that the Jews commence their *calendar days* in the evening is because **Jewish religious culture is primarily defined** by the cycles of the moon. The sun cannot be overlooked but their *primary symbolism* is lunar. **They measure** their days and months by the **cycles of the moon**, in accordance with their worship, anciently, of the <u>Moon god</u>, *Sin*. The moon, the symbol of the Semitic god of old, becomes readily visible at night, therefore they count their days from sunset, beginning with the first sighting of the *New Moon* as the *first day* of each month in turn.

Traditionally, Rosh Hashanah is seen as Judgment Day (Yom Hadin) by the Jews. They believe that, annually, on Yom Hadin (Rosh Hashanah) the books of Judgment are opened and each individual is judged in accordance with their actions of the previous year; **and also**, that the *span* in between

---

[18] I give comprehensive explanations of Mythological Parallels in *The Astrological Foundation Of The Christ Myth Book Four*

Section One

The Secret Origins Of Judaism

the *first day* of Tishri and the *tenth day* of Tishri, which date (Tishri 10) marks Yom Kippur i.e. the *Day of Atonement*, the fates of those judged will be sealed. **These ten days**, from Tishri 1 to Tishri 10, are referred to as the *Days of Awe* in keeping with Judaic traditions. **They cite three categories** in which the subjects are judged: **first** the *very righteous*, and the *very wicked*, who are rewarded or punished, as the case may be, immediately; **and then** there are the average people with some good as well as bad deeds to their charge, whose final judgment will be determined after evaluation up to the final hours of the *Day of Atonement*. **In a nutshell**, the three categories of those judged and sentenced by god under Judaic tradition are those declared as *Innocent* (righteous), and others judged as *Guilty* (wicked), and the remainder held *in limbo* (to be determined), whose fate is decided during the *ten days of awe*.

Judaic tradition holds that the world was created by god on the date of *Tishri one* i.e. Rosh Hashanah, and *final divine judgment* awaits us on this same date at some time in the future, when universal judgment occurs. I have little doubt that the Jews inherited or otherwise acquired this custom of *linking* the New Year and Judgment Day from the ancient Babylonians. **The Babylonians** observed their New Year in the Spring, proximate the vernal equinox, in the month of Nissanu. **The Babylonians believed**, religiously, that the fate of the world was decided each **New Year**; that the gods gathered in their cosmic heaven in the *"Room of Fate"* and decided the Judgment (Fate) of the world.

Tishri, Month of Lunar-Solar Reconciliation

It is important to note, Rosh Hashanah <u>does not mark</u> the anniversary of the <u>solar year</u>, that is to say, the tropical year of approximately 365 days. Rosh Hashanah marks the renewal of the <u>lunar</u> year at close to 354 days, which runs short of the solar year by about eleven days. From Rosh Hashanah to Rosh Hashanah, as transmitted in the written Torah or bible, marks a lunar year of about 354 days. By inserting a 13th month into their calendar at roughly 3 year intervals the Hebrews are able to calibrate the lunar cycle of about 354 days with the solar cycle of about 365 days to a

Section One

The Secret Origins Of Judaism

significant degree. **However** the method of reconciling the Lunar year to the Solar year is not given in the bible. Of course, the whole purpose of this lunar-solar calibration process is to keep the months of the Hebrew lunar calendar in sync with the seasons which (seasons) are governed by the solar cycle - **the net result of all these** calendar tweakings is that the Jewish festivals will remain in season.

The current modern Jewish calendar inserts an extra month seven times, at predetermined intervals, over a 19 year cycle, so as to keep the calendar and seasons of the year in harmony. The Hebrews of old could not have kept their festivals in sync with the seasons by use of the lunar calendar only; that is, without some means of adjusting their calendar to account for the discrepancy between the lunar and solar years, as noted in the previous paragraph. A mathematical method for tracking the lunar cycles or adjusting the lunar calendar to the solar cycle by the use of mathematical formulas or calculations *is not given* in the Torah. Being that the ancient Hebrews made adjustments or intercalations to their calendar *in response to their observations* of the cosmos and Mother Nature, a calculated calendar system was not necessary.

For some centuries now, the Jews have used a calendar that incorporates the Metonic system whereby the lunar calendar is calibrated to the solar annual cycle with intercalary adjustments made seven times within a nineteen year *Metonic* cycle. The *current* Judaic calendar, *by calculation*, inserts an extra month of 29 or 30 days in the 3rd, 6th, 8th, 11th, 14th, 17th, and 19th years - and by this method, the Jewish festivals are kept in tune with the seasons; however, anciently, neither the Metonic system or other available calculative systems were used by the Hebrews to *predict* the appearances of the New Moons and subsequently track the months and seasons - rather they relied on empirical *observations* of the moon cycles as they unfolded.

According to Judaic religious tradition the months do not commence until the New Moon is actually *seen, witnessed, and confirmed* by the Sanhedrin or Rabbis. The requirement for actually viewing the birth of the New Moon

Section One

The Secret Origins Of Judaism

was sacred amongst the Jews, hence by tradition, each New Moon had to be officially announced to the faithful before recognition of a new month was acceptable.

The purpose of the Metonic calendar or system is to provide the Jews with a formula by which they can periodically insert an extra lunar month into the year, and thereby keep their months from drifting out of season, *without the need to actually observe* the moon cycles. **Anciently**, even before the adoption of the Metonic mathematical formula that they now use, **they had to follow the same** or *similar* methods of intercalation, in order to keep their months in sync with the seasons. **The difference was**, that they made the adjustments or intercalations *in response to factors noted by their observations*; that is to say, *when or after they noticed* through observation that the calendar was drifting out of season, *they would then*, in response, make the necessary calendrical tweaks to keep the calendar and their festivals in sync with the seasons.

In other words, when they *observed*, for instance, that the crop cycles were not in sync with the calendar, and that the seasons were drifting away from the appropriate calendar dates, they would, *in response* to their observations, make the necessary adjustments to their calendar by the use of *Festival Sabbaths,* a Festival Sabbath being a non-counted day(s) or intercalated day(s), in compliance with the situation at hand; or they would create a lunar leap year by inserting an additional month (Adar 2) toward the end of the adjusted year, thus creating a lunar leap year of thirteen months.

Also, the ancient Jewish calendar required that the *first New Moon* of the *religious year*, that is to say the 1st day of the month of Nissan, occur as the first New Moon *after* the passing of the vernal equinox - so if they *observed* that Nissan 1 was coming before the vernal equinox, such an occasion signaled that the time may have arrived to intercalate a 13th month into their calendar so as to keep the month of Nissan in accord with the seasons.

The Ancients used *various* means to keep the lunar calendar in sync with the tropical year, we need not try to detail most or all of these methods. The important factor is that all of the older methods were dependant upon

Section One

The Secret Origins Of Judaism

observations (as also required by the Jewish faith) of the skies for signs or indicators of when to adjust the calendar, and likewise *observations of the cyclical trends in nature* such as crop cycles and animal migrations, which trends are precise, and dictated by nature's ever ticking clock.

We have stressed and emphasized the *observational aspect* of the old Jewish calendar so as to differentiate the old calendar system from the current Jewish calendar. The old calendar relied on the results of witnessed observations of the New Moon as signals for the cycles of the months, as determined by the phases of the moon. The current Judaic calendar, which was essentially put in place in the early centuries of our present era, is based on a mathematical formula (Metonic calculation) that *predicts* the occurrences of the New Moon. The calendar is not affected by human observations or fractional late or early returns of the New Moon relative to the calendar, because the phases tend to average out during the full *nineteen year term* of the formula's cycle.

A calendar that relied on observations worked fine for the Hebrews when they were a small regional community in and about Jerusalem. They could, with relative ease, sight the New moon as it appeared each month - pass the word on to the governing Jewish clergy, the Sanhedrin, who would certify the sighting, and in turn send out messengers and/or messages of various modes to notify the general Jewish community that Rosh Hodesh (1st day of a new month) had officially arrived, that the *New Moon* had, again, been *born*.

However, this observational system had its limits, and was not practicable or efficiently operable for the Hebrews, over the advancing centuries, as their tribe expanded, and portions of the population migrated to distant lands, and the Hebrew people became multi-regional, dispersed to far-flung communities throughout the known world. **The old calendar system required** that Rosh Hodesh, the birth of the New Moon, could not be certified until **confirmation** by the central clerical authority of Jerusalem; **this became unworkable** when Jews became widely dispersed and out of close contact with Jerusalem. And being that the appearance of the New

Section One

The Secret Origins Of Judaism

Moon *varied* in distant lands, and even the time of day varied between locations separated by significant degrees of longitude, they were compelled to adopt a calculative system that was *suitable for any location* in the world; hence they were eventually driven to adopt the *calculated calendar* so as to efficiently serve the ever expanding worldwide Jewish community.

Our discussion of the particulars of the Judaic calendar are very important, because the vaunted Jewish calendar is central to Judaism as the prime holder and regulator of the *alleged covenant* between the Jews and god. The covenant, as we have shown above, is inextricably linked to the Seven Jewish Feasts; and these feasts, of course, are regulated by the Judaic calendar. Also, An efficiently working Judaic calendar was essential to preserving the cultural unity of the Jewish people. The timely observances of the **Seven Jewish Festivals** are integral to their faith. The dispersed Jewish people could not remain in true cultural and religious harmony without a genuine but **updated** Jewish calendar that kept them in compliance with their assorted covenantal obligations. Their Judaic rituals had to remain synchronized and standardized, per god's decree, that is according to Judaic religious doctrine. In order for the Jews to remain culturally and religiously bonded, they needed a calendar that kept the Jewish people in harmony with the Judaic festivals, regardless of the varied geographical locations of the burgeoning and widely scattered Jewish populations.

It begs to be remembered that the precise recognition of the birth of the New Moon carries *important religious significance* amongst the Hebrews, who were, in fact, ancient worshippers of the *moon god*, Sin (Sin as in Mt. Sin-ai). The reverential regard of *Rosh Hodesh*, that is to say the New Moon, at its resurgence into light from out of the womb of cosmic darkness is comparable to the observance of the Sabbath, or nearly so according to the dictates of the bible - note the following: *Isaiah 66:23 And it shall come to pass, that from one <u>new moon</u> to another, and from one sabbath to another, shall all flesh come to worship before me, saith the LORD. Ezekiel 46:1 Thus saith the Lord GOD; The gate of the inner court that looketh toward the east shall be shut the six working days; but on the sabbath it shall be opened, and in the day of the <u>new moon</u>*

Section One

The Secret Origins Of Judaism

it shall be opened. Colossians 2:16 Let no man therefore judge you in meat, or in drink, or in respect of an holyday, or of the <u>new moon</u>, or of the sabbath days:
The Metonic *calculated* calendar did not evolve, with certainty, amongst the Jews until the Common Era. Various dates are given for the commencement of the efforts of reform that led to the *Reformed Jewish Calendar,* which, of course, incorporates the Metonic system. It's pretty well certain that the process of reform was commenced by the third century CE, or slightly before, and completed officially, but nevertheless tentatively, to its more or less modern form by the fifth century of our present Era; with adjustments and tweaks done to the calendar, over the centuries, as initiated and/or sanctioned by the Rabbis, although opinions differ on the precise chronological evolution of the Judaic calendar.

It is not precisely clear how the Jews reconciled the lunar and solar cycles anciently, that is, before enacting the calendar reforms in the early centuries of our Common Era - **they did not record their methods** of *lunar-solar reconciliation* in their scriptures, that is to say the bible or Written Torah. Whether they adjusted the calendar to some degree *yearly* or more significantly at intervals of two to three *years* is not precisely known, according to scholars that have researched these matters.

Actually, it's not important, for our immediate purposes within this essay, that we know *exactly* how the Hebrews calibrated their lunar calendar to the solar cycle in those bygone days. **The important factor** is that the Hebrews were periodically *prompted* to make adjustments to their calendar whenever their observations detected that the calendar was drifting out of sync with the seasons; because the *most important function* of the calendar was to mark the dates for planting and harvesting.

As we have noted continuously in our essay, **we reject** the Jewish assertion that the Jewish calendar and feasts were ordained by god; hence, all facts that help cement the intimate connection of the Jewish calendar with mundane agricultural functions lends credence to our claim that these festivals had no bona fide religious affiliations when originally conceived. **The spurious religious veneer** was applied later, after and during the

Section One

The Secret Origins Of Judaism

evolution of the Judaic religious concepts amongst the previously pagan Hebrews.

We know that they kept their calendar tuned to the seasons by *methods of observation* - observations of the sun as well as the moon; and also observations of their natural habitat - for instance if they noticed that their calendar was not in tune with an agricultural cycle by reason of a plant's budding or ripening, such was an indication that their calendar was in need of a special adjustment. **They were able to note the seasons** by observing the ascents and descents of certain stars and/or constellations, and also the changing declinations of the sun throughout the year. **We know** that the calendar was adjusted at intervals, and that a council of Rabbis (Sanhedrin) was the traditionally and biblically sanctioned authority for making adjustments (intercalations and such) to **their calendar**.

It is evident that the Rabbis did not keep *public* records of the methods employed to reconcile the lunar calendar with the annual solar cycle. This is because the adjustments were done on an ad hoc basis by the Rabbis, resultant from *each instance* of the pertinent solar observations. The solar-lunar reconciliations were enacted when their (Rabbis) *observations revealed the need* for a calendrical adjustment. **In other words**, a judgment call was made by the Rabbis, based on solar *observations*, not calculations; an edict was sent out to the Jewish community by the Rabbis as to the stipulated calendrical adjustments - thus the lunar calendar was adjusted or reconciled with the tropical cycle for the year in question.

Rosh Hashanah is the Jewish New Year, but it is not noted as the beginning of the year in the bible, neither is it mentioned as the End of the Year. Rosh Hashanah falls on the *first day of the seventh month* of the Jewish lunar calendar - it has been designated by the Rabbis as the Head of the Year, or the New Years Day of the Hebrews.

The bible designates Rosh Hashanah as a *Sabbath*; by implication, that means that this day was dedicated to god with the same or nearly the same fervor as the weekly *Saturday* Sabbath. Take note of the following bible verses: *Leviticus 23:24 Speak unto the children of Israel, saying, In the seventh*

Section One

The Secret Origins Of Judaism

month, in the first day of the month, shall ye have a sabbath, a memorial of blowing of trumpets, an holy convocation. Numbers 29:1 *And in the seventh month, on the first day of the month, ye shall have an holy convocation; ye shall do no servile work: it is a day of blowing the trumpets unto you.*

Rosh Hashanah, also known as **Yom Hadin** (Judgment Day) is followed *ten days later*, on Tishri 10, by **Yom Kippur**, that is, the *Day of Atonement*; and then another five days later on Tishri 15 falls **Sukkoth**, which commences the last harvest of the Jewish year - the fruit harvest.... Take note of the following biblical passages **that signify Sukkoth as the End of the Jewish year:** *Exodus 23:16 And the feast of harvest, the firstfruits of thy labours, which thou hast sown in the field: and the feast of ingathering, which is in the end of the year, when thou hast gathered in thy labours out of the field. Exodus 34:22 And thou shalt observe the feast of weeks, of the firstfruits of wheat harvest, and the feast of ingathering at the year's end.*

It is significant that the bible refers to Sukkoth on Tishri 15 as the end of the year, and not to Rosh Hashanah on Tishri 1. **This indicates**, among other possibilities, that the period of the seven festivals *from Passover to Sukkoth* was seen as an agricultural season or *agricultural year of seven months*, **as it were**, which was ended with the last harvest of **the agrarian year**, namely Sukkoth.

The rainy season commenced after the fruit harvest of Sukkoth; also, they entered into the five months of Fall-Winter sequestration or retrenchment, till the arrival of the month of Nisan at the first New moon after the vernal equinox. The month of Nisan brings relief from the **afflictions of winter** and marks the beginning of Spring and the advent of Passover, which is the first of the seven annual Jewish feasts.

As already noted, **Passover symbolizes** the passing of the sun over the vernal equinox, and its **liberation** from its *cosmic bondage* in the underworld (lower hemisphere) into its fullness of potency and liberty in the upper hemisphere, signified by the atmospheric dominance of the sun during the Spring and Summer.

Section One

The Secret Origins Of Judaism

Lunar year solar year - Jubilee

It behooves us, at this point, to discuss briefly the Jubilee Year. The Jewish New Year of Tishri 1 is a *lunar year* of about 354 days, as we have noted above. Without adjustments being made to the Jewish calendar, their months would lose calibrations with the seasons, so **it is an absolute** *impossibility* that the Jewish lunar-solar calendar ever functioned without some sort of interplay with a solar calendar or reckoning so as to keep the *months* in season; and thereby the *festivals* in season. The methods that the Hebrews used in some ancient eras have not come down to us, therefore, in some cases, we have to connect the dots, so to speak, from the information which is available.

We know that the original purpose of the Jewish festivals was the tracking of time so as to regulate planting and harvesting, and other mundane activities; **therefore**, when seeking to decipher *why* certain festivals are stationed at certain dates, we always look first for reasons related to *time tracking*.

It is certain that the festival of **Yom Kippur**, in its origination, was a marker of the end of the *solar* year or the approaching of the end of the solar year. **We know**, likewise for certain, that the ancients used or dallied with a calendar of 364 days to the year (at times called a Jubilee Year of 364 days), with one uncounted day or holiday appended so as to match the solar year of 365 days.

Yom Kippur, at ten days after Tishri 1, *fits perfectly* as a *marker* for the **solar year completion**. Rosh Hashanah marks a lunar year of 354 days - with 10 days added to the count at Yom Kippur makes approximately a solar year of 364 days. **The span of 5 days** between *Yom Kippur and Sukkoth* allowed the ancient Hebrews an ample span of days to intercalate one or two days as needed **to complete the solar year at 365 or 366 days.**

It is a certainty, as evidence clearly indicates, that the interval in between Tishri 10 i.e. Yom Kippur, and Tishri 15 i.e. Sukkoth provided the Jews with a window of time by which to calibrate the lunar and solar years, *by*

Section One

95

The Secret Origins Of Judaism

notation possibly, in an ad hoc fashion, for any year, be it regular or Leap year. **The same holds true for the 5 day period between Nisan 10 and Nisan 15** - on Nisan 10 the sacrificial lamb is selected and on Nisan 15, the Passover is observed. **So the Jews have situated the Vernal and Autumnal festivals** as mirrored reflections of each other so that what ever holds as calendrical truth for one also holds true for the other.

The bible itself correlates the Jubilee year of 364 days with the event of Yom Kippur, as I have suggested above. The Jubilee years were *solar years, not lunar years,* that the Semites reconciled or celebrated at fifty year intervals with special religious and cultural observances. **The bible states** clearly that the *7th month and the 10th day* of the month was the anniversary for the *year of the Jubilee.* **I think** that this provides explicit proof that the festival of Yom Kippur, which falls in the 7th month on the tenth day, was a marker for the completion of the solar year - please note:........*Leviticus 25:9 Then shalt thou cause the trumpet of the **jubile** to sound on the **tenth day of the seventh month**, in the day of atonement shall ye make the trumpet sound throughout all your land.* **The bible clearly indicates** that the anniversary of the Jubilee Year was set at the festival of Yom Kippur, **which measures a Solar Year of 364 days.** This is extremely significant as an indicator of *why* both equinoxes have markers spaced ten days from the opening day of the year. Of course, the Jubilee year required an epagomenal Sabbath Day appended to make the actual solar year of 365 days.

Of course, the only way to keep the lunar calendar *itself* in sync with the seasons was by adjusting the calendar periodically by the insertion of a month every two to three years per the Metonic cycle, or by some other system of intercalation. **The Metonic cycle is not the only method** by which the lunar year can be reconciled to the solar year. **The bible is silent** on just how the Jews reconciled the lunar and solar years, before the enactment of the Metonic system by the Rabbis in the Common Era.

There is no disputing the fact that under the biblical system or calendar, the beginnings of their lunar months were based on observations, and announced at the time the New Moon had been sighted and verified by

Section One

The Secret Origins Of Judaism

witnesses; **so it follows logically**, that the *solar years were not calculated either*, but, as with the lunar cycle, noted by observations of the locations of the sun, when it crossed a certain gauge, celestial or man-made that indicated the annual solar cycle was complete - **hence** the annual cycles of the sun could have been kept annotatively in their calendrical records. **Consequently** they could have made adjustments or intercalations to their lunar calendar, by Rabbinical edicts, as dictated by circumstances, and, of course, records of such ad hoc adjustments would not come down to us.

The association of Yom Kippur with the *approach* and/or *ending* of the solar year was a matter of notation or annotation if you will, done each year, so as to properly track the sun's cycle. **It is readily understandable** that ad hoc annotations to the calendar would not be kept in the regular calendrical record and passed down within the public domain - that we can reasonably surmise. **Be that as it may**, the actual adjustment of the lunar calendar so that the lunar months were kept in sync with the seasons could have been done only by periodic intercalations (such as a 13th month inserted every 2 to 3 years) to the lunar calendar so that the months matched the seasons.

An example of the 364-day year is in *game symbolism* that has come down to us over the years. **Playing Cards carry calendar symbolism.** A deck of Poker Playing Cards consist of 52+2 cards; the cards have 4 Suits - each Suit has 13 units; there are 12 Face Cards in the deck. **Throughout the centuries** various sages have implanted signs and symbols within our environs; in literature, graphically, architecturally, in dramas, plays, and games, that are symbolic of profound ancient truths - such is the case with Playing Cards relative to the seasons and the years.

The symbolism is as follows: The **four suits** of the cards signify the four seasons, the **thirteen numbers** of each suit from 1 (the Ace) to 13 (the King) are for the 13 weeks to each season. **The weeks** of all four seasons (4 times 13) total to 52 weeks for the year. **The three face cards** of each suit are for the signs of the zodiac including the Cardinal signs (Kings), the Fixed signs (Queens), and the Mutable signs (Jacks) - the total of 12 face cards matches the 12 signs of the zodiac. Multiply the 52 weeks by 7 and the

Section One

The Secret Origins Of Judaism

result is 364 days to the year, as I indicated above - **this is the Jubilee year** used by some of the ancients. Of course there are **actually** 365 days to the year regularly **and** 366 days to the year during Leap years - **this circumstance is covered** by the 2 Jokers which float through the deck (year) as needed. One Joker is added to make the 364-day year fit the solar cycle of 365 days, and of course, the purpose of the 2nd Joker is for adding 2 days so as **to fit the Leap Year** of 366 days.

At this point we shall include the festival of Yom Kippur in our continuing analysis of the three Judaic Fall Festivals.

Yom Kippur

Yom Kippur is the *great day* of the *Jewish year*, it marks the Day of Atonement, when the faithful Jews turn toward their god, beseeching forgiveness for their sins of the previous year. Yom Kippur is observed on **Tishri 10**; Tishri is the seventh month of the Jewish lunar year. It is a day of Fasting, Prayer, and Penitence - the faithful Fast for the entire day of Yom Kippur; they congregate in their synagogues bowed in meditation, prayer, and chanting. Yom Kippur is the most sacred day of the Jewish calendar....*Leviticus 16:29-31 And this shall be a statute for ever unto you: that in the seventh month, on the tenth day of the month, ye shall afflict your souls, and do no work at all, whether it be one of your own country, or a stranger that sojourneth among you: For on that day shall the priest make an atonement for you, to cleanse you, that ye may be clean from all your sins before the LORD. It shall be a sabbath of rest unto you, and ye shall afflict your souls, by a statute for ever.*

Judaic doctrine teaches that Rosh Hashanah, ten days before Yom Kippur, marks the day of divine judgment. **The Hebrews believe** that, annually, on the first day of the month of Tishri, **the books of Judgment are opened**, called *The Book Of Life*, and each individual is judged in accordance with their actions of the previous year. **The Book of Life** is said to remain open for ten days, that is from Rosh Hashanah to Yom Kippur. **These ten days**, from Tishri 1 to Tishri 10, are referred to as the *Days of Awe* in keeping with Judaic traditions. **Those who are judged** appear before god in three

Section One

The Secret Origins Of Judaism

categories, the *blessed*, the *damned*, and the *purgatorial* - the purgatorial refers to those penitents whose fate has yet to be decided. Yom Kippur is given as the last chance, the last day for those whose fate is in abeyance, to make things right with god, that is to atone for their sins.

Anciently, according to Jewish lore, Yom Kippur was the day, *the only day*, in which the **Holy of Holies** of the Tabernacle or Jerusalem Temple was entered - it was entered by the High Priest only, others were not allowed to enter on this date of Yom Kippur or on any other date. The Holy of Holies was a dark windowless room that faced due east - **inside this room** was placed the Ark of the Covenant, topped off by a *Mercy Seat* no less, on which god seated himself! according to Jewish doctrine. **If we are to believe** the bible, this room was constructed as a place for god to meet with his chosen - **take note of the following verses:**... *Exodus 25:21-22 And thou shalt put the mercy seat above upon the ark; and in the ark thou shalt put the testimony that I shall give thee. And there I will meet with thee, and I will commune with thee from above the mercy seat, from between the two cherubims which are upon the ark of the testimony, of all things which I will give thee in commandment unto the children of Israel. ...Leviticus 16:2 And the LORD said unto Moses, Speak unto Aaron thy brother, that he come not at all times into the holy place within the vail before the mercy seat, which is upon the ark; that he die not: for I will appear in the cloud upon the mercy seat....* And as we continue: *Numbers 7:89 And when Moses was gone into the tabernacle of the congregation to speak with him, then he heard the voice of one speaking unto him from off the mercy seat that was upon the ark of testimony, from between the two cherubims: and he spake unto him. Numbers 8:1 **And the LORD spake unto Moses, saying**,...Exodus 25:8 And let them make me a sanctuary; that I may dwell among them....Exodus 29:42-43 This shall be a continual burnt offering throughout your generations at the door of the tabernacle of the congregation before the LORD: where I will meet you, to speak there unto thee. And there I will meet with the children of Israel, and the tabernacle shall be sanctified by my glory........***The biblical verses just presented** suggest to us that the **lord god** of the universe instructed his chosen to construct, for him, **an earthly throne** from which he, god, could commune with his earthly subjects. **I must interject** at this point - as a *rational person*, **I cannot bring myself to understand** how any right-

Section One

The Secret Origins Of Judaism

minded, lucid individual could accept these verses as literal truth; that is, that the lord god of the universe has need or desire for an earthly residence, to serve as his headquarters or ambassadorial residence, so to speak. **Of course if one admits** that the verses are *not believable* as presented, then such an admission is tantamount to admitting that **the bible is a fraud**, that is to say, *not* the word of god. **Undoubtedly**, such an admission would leave monotheism in the lurch - **exposed and invalidated**, as *should be* the case in my opinion.

The great goal of Yom Kippur is mercy and forgiveness, the faithful Hebrews want, perhaps above everything else, to be spared from the wrath of god - this is made plain in the explanation and bible verses cited above. The picture painted of god by the biblical verses I have inserted above is quite fantastic, in fact, *unbelievable* in my opinion. **First off**, if you believe it! god, as stated in these verses speaks to us in the *first person*, quote: "*I will commune with thee from above the mercy seat*" and if you swallow that, it follows that god's appearance was in the form of a mist or cloud hovering above the mercy seat within the room called the Holy of Holies - such is stated in the biblical verses I have included above.

As before noted, Yom Kippur, the Day of Atonement, is the most precious of all the Jewish holidays or Sabbath days, appointed for them by god almighty, according to Jewish doctrine. **We, of course, do not accept the Jewish assertion** of godly endorsement for their so-called sacred days, and this essay is dedicated to the *unveiling* of the unbridled deceit embedded within that assertion, that is to say, the implausible claim of divine sanction and concordance for Jewish holy days.

In order to link Yom Kippur with its true primitive origins, we must explore the festival of Yom Kippur *as biblically represented* as well as the popular Rabbinic version now so popularly commemorated by the Jewish populations of the world. There are differences between the original Yom Kippur of the bible, and the refined version touted by the Rabbis. Our pathway to the pagan origins of the festival is routed by way of the biblical Yom Kippur, which we shall explore in due course. The modern festival of

Section One

The Secret Origins Of Judaism

Yom Kippur is solidly focused on redemption, penitence, and mercy, which, to my opinion, is fine and laudable.

The currently popular or modern rituals of Yom Kippur have been constructed and systemized by the Jewish clergy, under *Rabbinic Judaism*; **however, it is within the bible, itself**, under *biblical Judaism* that we shall find step by step instructions on how Yom Kippur should be observed, in accordance with the command of Yahweh, the Jewish god. The rituals of the bible, which we shall explore, involve much bloodshed and seemingly bizarre behavior - it is through the bible version of Yom Kippur that we can, by historical associations with ancient pagan rites, unveil the pagan origins of this Jewish holy day. **First**, in order to enhance our understanding and comprehension of the Jewish *Fall* (autumn) feasts of *Rosh Hashanah*, *Yom Kippur*, and, soon to be reviewed, *Sukkoth*, **let us review the following excerpt from my book** *The Astrological Foundation Of The Christ Myth Book Four*, wherein I give a summary of *Festivals 5, 6, and 7* - the Jewish Autumn festivals. This may be a bit redundant but I think it's important...

"**5 - Rosh Hashanah:** This is the Hebrew New Year, also referred to as Judgment Day, as trumpets are blown to recognize this month of destiny. It is the 7th month and 1st day of the Religious year that commences in the month of Nisan and/or it is the 1st month and 1st day of the Jewish civil year i.e. Tishri 1......**Leviticus 23:23 through Leviticus 23:25** - ^{23}*And the LORD spake unto Moses, saying,* ^{24}*Speak unto the children of Israel, saying, In the seventh month, in the first day of the month, shall ye have a sabbath, a memorial of blowing of trumpets, an holy convocation.* ^{25}*Ye shall do no servile work therein: but ye shall offer an offering made by fire unto the LORD.........*Some interesting characteristics of **Rosh Hashanah** include the blowing of the Shofar horn, as a warning or announcement that Judgment Day (Rosh Hashanah) has arrived. Jewish tradition dictates that Rosh Hashanah is annually the Judgment Day – that on this day god judges his subjects and enters their names into a book that is called The Book Of Life. Rosh Hashanah commences ten days of penitence wherein the devout are obligated to seek forgiveness for their sins of the previous year and even ask forgiveness of those whom they may have wronged. After the ten days

Section One

The Secret Origins Of Judaism

have passed, on the evening of Yom Kippur, the Book Of Life is sealed and the fate of the subjects is destined. The Shofar horn is then blown to announce the sealing of the Book Of Life and the closing of the Days Of Awe, which is the term that collectively describes Rosh Hashanah and Yom Kippur.......**6 - Yom Kippur:** This is the Day Of Atonement, a day of prayer and repentance to the Jewish deity. It falls on the 10th day after the Jewish New Year. *Rosh Hashanah* commences 10 days of Penitence which climaxes on Tishri 10 on the day of Yom Kippur i.e. the Day Of Atonement. The Shofar (Ram's Horn) is associated with Yom Kippur. *Rosh Hashanah* also known as *Yom Hadin*, which means Day Of Judgment. Rosh Hashanah means *Head* of the year...Leviticus 23:27 through Leviticus 23:28 *^{27}Also on the tenth day of this seventh month there shall be a day of atonement: it shall be an holy convocation unto you; and ye shall afflict your souls, and offer an offering made by fire unto the LORD. ^{28}And ye shall do no work in that same day: for it is a day of atonement, to make an atonement for you before the LORD your god.* **7 - Sukkoth: This is the Feast Of Tabernacles**, a harvest festival commemorating the booths (temporary dwellings) in which the Israelites resided during their wandering in the wilderness, according to the myth..............................*Leviticus 23:33 through Leviticus 23:36* *^{33}And the LORD spake unto Moses, saying, ^{34}Speak unto the children of Israel, saying, The fifteenth day of this seventh month shall be the feast of tabernacles for seven days unto the LORD. ^{35}On the first day shall be an holy convocation: ye shall do no servile work therein. ^{36}Seven days ye shall offer an offering made by fire unto the LORD: on the eighth day shall be an holy convocation unto you; and ye shall offer an offering made by fire unto the LORD: it is a solemn assembly; and ye shall do no servile work therein.* **Simchat Torah:** The closing of the Jewish festival season is the *Simchat Torah*, which means rejoicing in the Torah. This is observed at the closing of the 7-8 day Sukkoth festivities. Jewish tradition calls for the weekly reading of the Torah in the synagogue throughout the year. The readings are proportioned so as to complete simultaneously with the end of Sukkoth.

Section One

The Secret Origins Of Judaism

Simchat Torah is the reading of the last verses of the Torah for the year and the immediate commencement of the first reading of the new yearly cycle. The cycle of Torah readings begins with Genesis and runs through Deuteronomy by the end of the annual cycle of readings; thus completing the so-called five books of Moses - Genesis, Exodus, Leviticus, Numbers and Deuteronomy."

The information above gives us good insight into the traditional observances of the three Autumn feasts of the Jews, as formulated by the Jewish Rabbis; inclusive of Yom Kippur, which is now the focus of our investigation. Old Judaism, or perhaps I should say biblical Judaism, was for all practical purposes, a *Temple cult* focused on the alleged House of god, that is to say, the Temple in Jerusalem. The Temple was the focal point of each day's activity - the life of the whole Jewish community centered on the Temple, we are told. This is wholly understandable, *if* we are able to digest the biblical narrative that the Temple was *actually* the dwelling place of the lord of the universe, with the lord, god (Yahweh) seated in isolation within the confines of the Holy of Holies in the form of a ghostly mist. **According to the biblical quotations** handed down to us by the Jews, that I have cited above, **god dwelled there**, morphed into a cloud like form, **hovering** over the Mercy Seat, upon the Ark within the room named the Holy of Holies: *"for I[god] will appear in the cloud upon the mercy seat"* - see Leviticus 16:2.

Biblical Judaism, to a great extent is centered around the Temple of Jerusalem. As noted in the biblical verses above, god instructed the Jews to build a tabernacle for him, a Temple in which he, god, could dwell and commune with the Jewish people. As the biblical narrative goes, the Temple at Jerusalem was built by god's command by the great King Solomon, son of King David. Further, the bible tells us that the Holy of Holies, *god's personal room* which was set off within the Temple compound, was only entered one time each year, on the day of Yom Kippur; and even then, only the High Priest was allowed to enter the room. This was the biblical instruction - entrance only one time a year by the High Priest during the course of the Yom Kippur ceremonies. So **only the High Priest was**

Section One

The Secret Origins Of Judaism

allowed to look upon this misty god hovering within the Temple, and the viewing was limited to one session a year.

Be that as it may, the Temple complex was a *very active place* indeed - sacrifices, prayers, and rituals were *conducted daily* at the Temple in submission and atonement to God. All of the myriad Jewish rituals and ceremonies revolved in some way about the Temple, wherein god resided. **There were two official Daily Sacrifices** done at the Temple each and every day; one at nine o'clock in the morning, and an evening sacrifice commenced at three o'clock in the afternoon. The copious bloodletting and gratuitous slaughtering of animals for sacrificial purposes, and the burning of animal flesh upon alters took place at the Temple daily, *as unabashedly reported in the bible* - and **this, they say was done by the command of god** almighty, resident as a cloud like form within the inner sanctum of the Temple. **Take note of Solomon's declaration** in regards to god's house:... 2 *Chronicles 2:4 Behold, I build an house to the name of the LORD my god, to dedicate it to him, and to <u>burn before him sweet incense,</u> and for the continual shewbread, and for the <u>burnt offerings</u> <u>morning and evening,</u> on the <u>sabbaths,</u> and on the <u>new moons,</u> and on the <u>solemn feasts</u> of the LORD our god. <u>This is an ordinance for ever</u> to Israel*

The rituals of the Tabernacle or the Jerusalem Temple, as directed by the Torah, were precise and intricate, and not accepting of deviation. **The Levites were put in charge** of the ritualistic endeavors, **with orders to kill** anyone that violated the sanctuary....*Numbers 18:6-7 And I, behold, I have taken your brethren the Levites from among the children of Israel: to you they are given as a gift for the LORD, to do the service of the tabernacle of the congregation. Therefore thou and thy sons with thee shall keep your priest's office for every thing of the altar, and within the vail; and ye shall serve: I have given your priest's office unto you as a service of gift: and the stranger that cometh nigh shall be <u>put to death</u>*.

The ceremonies of the biblical Yom Kippur followed ageless traditions, descended to the Semitic peoples, probably, by way of the ancient non-Semitic Sumerians. The biblical Yom Kippur is presided over by the High

Section One

The Secret Origins Of Judaism

Priest, who is typed as a descendant of the first High Priest Aaron, the loyal brother/disciple of Moses.

The commencement of Yom Kippur ceremonies begin with confessions of sin - first, the High Priest must confess his own sins and the sins of his family. The sacrificial animals have already been gathered, that is the bull, ram and goats, and are at hand, prepped and ready to be offered sacrificially unto Yahweh. The entire congregation of Jews are gathered there at the Temple, in the vicinity of the sacrificial alter, with the High Priest. The High Priest now lays his hand upon the head of the sacrificial bull and profusely recites confessional prayers unto Yahweh. The High Priest admits the errors of himself and his family and begs for forgiveness - note the following:.......*Leviticus 16:3-6 Thus shall Aaron come into the holy place: with a young bullock for a sin offering, and a ram for a burnt offering. He shall put on the holy linen coat, and he shall have the linen breeches upon his flesh, and shall be girded with a linen girdle, and with the linen mitre shall he be attired: these are holy garments; therefore shall he wash his flesh in water, and so put them on. And he shall take of the congregation of the children of Israel two kids of the goats for a sin offering, and one ram for a burnt offering. And Aaron shall offer his bullock of the sin offering, which is for himself, and make an atonement for himself, and for his house.*

Next the High Priests calls forth from his menagerie two sacrificial goats, as blood sacrifices for the lord Yahweh. But the procedure for this sacrifice has a quirk of sorts - a way has been made for the release of one of the goats, to be spared, but nevertheless serve as a scapegoat for the sins of the Jews. The priest takes to pebbles or flakes, what have you, and marks one for god and the other for release i.e. the scapegoat. He shuffles the markers so that he can not discern between the two markers, and allows fate to decide which goat shall be sacrificed and which shall be released - to the wilderness. The choice made, the one goat is garnered for the slaughter, while the other goat is set aside, in reserve, awaiting release...... see the following: ....*Leviticus 16:7-10 And he shall take the two goats, and present them before the LORD at the door of the tabernacle of the congregation. And Aaron shall cast lots upon the two goats; one lot for the LORD, and the other lot for the scapegoat. And Aaron shall bring the goat upon which the LORD'S lot fell, and*

Section One

The Secret Origins Of Judaism

offer him for a sin offering. But the goat, on which the lot fell to be the scapegoat, shall be presented alive before the LORD, to make an atonement with him, and to let him go for a scapegoat into the wilderness.

At this time, The High Priest and his aids set their eyes upon the bull or bullock, there in waiting - they slaughter the animal, prep it as their rituals prescribe. **They take a container of the animal's blood**, along with burning coals, and smoking incense and proceed toward the entrance to the *Holy of Holies* i.e. the sanctuary of god. While the assistants pause, the High Priest pushes aside the veil that covers the entrance to the Holy of Holies and he alone enters - he takes with him the fiery coals and smoking incense and places these items into the room before the seat of Yahweh, the misty god shrouded in cloud-like form, that resides therein - **the High Priest takes the container of blood, dips his fingers into it** repeatedly as he sprinkles blood about the environs in a designed ritualistic pattern - take note of the following:.......*Leviticus 16:11-14 And Aaron shall bring the bullock of the sin offering, which is for himself, and shall make an atonement for himself, and for his house, and shall kill the bullock of the sin offering which is for himself: And he shall take a censer full of burning coals of fire from off the altar before the LORD, and his hands full of sweet incense beaten small, and bring it within the vail: And he shall put the incense upon the fire before the LORD, that the cloud of the incense may cover the mercy seat that is upon the testimony, that he die not: And he shall take of the blood of the bullock, and sprinkle it with his finger upon the mercy seat eastward; and before the mercy seat shall he sprinkle of the blood with his finger seven times.*

The killing is not yet done! - now the priests turn upon the goat previously chosen, by the casting of lots, as the sacrificial gift of atonement for the general Jewish population. They slaughter the animal and basically repeat the ritualistic processes that followed the slaughtering of the sacrificial bull - see the following:.......*Leviticus 16:15-19 Then shall he kill the goat of the sin offering, that is for the people, and bring his blood within the vail, and do with that blood as he did with the blood of the bullock, and sprinkle it upon the mercy seat, and before the mercy seat: And he shall make an atonement for the holy place, because of the uncleanness of the children of Israel, and because of their transgressions in all their sins: and so shall he do for the tabernacle of the*

Section One

The Secret Origins Of Judaism

congregation, that remaineth among them in the midst of their uncleanness. And there shall be no man in the tabernacle of the congregation when he goeth in to make an atonement in the holy place, until he come out, and have made an atonement for himself, and for his household, and for all the congregation of Israel. And he shall go out unto the altar that is before the LORD, and make an atonement for it; <u>and shall take of the blood of the bullock, and of the blood of the goat,</u> and put it upon the horns of the altar round about. And he shall <u>sprinkle</u> of the <u>blood</u> upon it with his finger seven times, and cleanse it, and hallow it from the uncleanness of the children of Israel.

We come now to the scapegoat, standing there trembling perhaps, in abeyance, awaiting its fate. The High Priest now proceeds toward the scapegoat, lays his hand upon its head, and repeats prayers of expiation for the people of Israel - that their sins are transferred to the scapegoat, and the scapegoat is thus released and escorted away from the proceedings into the wilderness - note the following:........*Leviticus 16:20-22 And when he hath made an end of reconciling the holy place, and the tabernacle of the congregation, and the altar, <u>he shall bring the live goat</u>: And Aaron shall lay both his hands upon the head of the live goat, and <u>confess over him</u> all the iniquities of the children of Israel, and all their transgressions in <u>all their sins</u>, putting them upon the head of the goat, and shall send him away by the hand of a fit man into the wilderness: And <u>the goat shall bear upon him all their iniquities</u> unto a land not inhabited: and he shall let go the goat in the wilderness.*

After the slaughtering is complete, the High Priest and his assistant priests doff their blood splattered garments, wash up, and put on fresh attire. They gather the scraps of skin, gristle, intestinal waste, bones, what have you; take the items to a spot and burn them - see the following:........*Leviticus 16:23-28 And Aaron shall come into the tabernacle of the congregation, and shall put off the linen garments, which he put on when he went into the holy place, and shall leave them there: And he shall wash his flesh with water in the holy place, and put on his garments, and come forth, and offer his burnt offering, and the burnt offering of the people, and make an atonement for himself, and for the people. And the fat of the sin offering shall he burn upon the altar. And he that let go the goat for the scapegoat shall wash his clothes, and bathe his flesh in water, and afterward come into the camp. And the bullock for the sin offering, and the goat for the sin offering, whose blood was brought in to make atonement in the holy place, shall one*

Section One

The Secret Origins Of Judaism

carry forth without the camp; and they shall burn in the fire their skins, and their flesh, and their dung. And he that burneth them shall wash his clothes, and bathe his flesh in water, and afterward he shall come into the camp.

The bloodletting rituals are an eternal *obligation* **of the Jews** - The congregation is now exhorted as to their obligations to God, of their covenant with god as a special people. **They are reminded** that *this ceremony of Yom Kippur must be repeated from year to year throughout all eternity,* **on the tenth day of the seventh month** - note the following:........*Leviticus 16:29-34 And this shall be a statute for ever unto you: that in the seventh month, on the tenth day of the month, ye shall afflict your souls, and do no work at all, whether it be one of your own country, or a stranger that sojourneth among you: For on that day shall the priest make an atonement for you, to cleanse you, that ye may be clean from all your sins before the LORD. It shall be a <u>sabbath</u> of rest unto you, and ye shall afflict your souls, by a statute for ever. And the priest, whom he shall anoint, and whom he shall consecrate to minister in the priest's office in his father's stead, shall make the <u>atonement</u>, and shall put on the linen clothes, even the holy garments: And he shall make an <u>atonement</u> for the <u>holy sanctuary</u>, and he shall make an <u>atonement</u> for the <u>tabernacle</u> of the <u>congregation</u>, and for the <u>altar</u>, and he shall make an atonement for the priests, and for all the people of the congregation. And this shall be an everlasting statute unto you, to make an atonement for the children of Israel for all their sins once a year. And he did as the LORD commanded Moses.*

This completes the biblical instruction for the Yom Kippur ceremony. The clergy tells us that the bizarre rituals that we have just reviewed were **established by godly decree** - that the bible is god's word. I think that it must be abundantly clear to all *truth seekers*, who possess the courage to weigh these matters dispassionately and unemotionally, that the Jewish claim of divine sponsorship cannot withstand rational scrutiny. The rituals that we have just examined are not only implausible and puzzling but also clearly and blatantly absurd. In regards to the Yom Kippur festival, and the other festivals that we have reviewed to this point, the taint of primitive sacrificial rites and superstitions is palpable. These so-called godly ordained religious rites are clearly holdovers from distant primal ages when the Semitic or Hebrew culture was grossly underdeveloped and very primitive.

Section One

The Secret Origins Of Judaism

The Judaic ritual sacrifices, and such, are not included in modern Rabbinical Judaism. The Jews claim that they stopped or *paused* the sacrificial bloodletting, as advocated in the bible, because the destruction of the Jerusalem Temple in A.D. 70 made such goings on impractical - such is the Jewish excuse or reason for not continuing the rituals *commanded* by the Torah. **I wonder**, should we therefore conclude that if the Temple had not been destroyed, that they, the Jews, would yet be conducting these bizarre bloodletting rituals - **and further**, if the Temple is ever rebuilt, as some claim it must be, so as to prepare for god's coming - will they again recommence those primitive bloodletting rituals? **If the Temple is rebuilt**, will Yahweh again take residence in the Temple sanctuary, in the form of a cloud, *hovering* above the Mercy Seat?

The Jerusalem Temple, with its sacred sanctuary and the Jewish god allegedly hovering in the Holy of Holies over the Mercy Seat, was central to the Yom Kippur and other Temple ceremonies. The procedures or rituals could not be accomplished properly without the traditional trappings and components of the Temple. **According to Jewish lore**, the Temple was twice destroyed, first in B.C. 586, and the final destruction in A.D. 70. As an aside, I should now point out for future reference that as our essays progress we will eventually revisit some aspects of the Temple Ritualism, pursuant to its mystical interpretations. Also, it is very interesting to note that the reputed planners or builders of the Temple i.e. King David and King Solomon are *mythical*, and *not* actually *historical* personalities.

The Rabbis have now, over the centuries, revised or reconstructed Judaism so as to make it a better fit for the modern world, and more intellectually palatable for the somewhat improved acumen of today's Jewish populations; be that as it may, I am not aware of any public repudiation of the base, primitive sacrificial rites promoted by the Torah/Bible. **The current form of Rabbinic Judaism** is centered around perpetuating the myth of specialness amongst the Jewish people through the ritualized readings of the Torah, the keeping of the modified seven Jewish Feasts, the Synagogue rituals, and their inherited cultural traditions.

Section One

The Secret Origins Of Judaism

Judaic religion, with its incessant rituals and ceremonies focused on the purported divine mission of the Jewish people is, in fact, a cult like, insidious but masterful, systematic **system of religious indoctrination** targeted at the Jewish Rank and File. Undoubtedly there are an abundant amount of Jews who *actually* believe that they are god's chosen race. Of course the *wiser* Jews know that Judaism is a farce, *as literally presented*. **The Judaic methodology** has fostered a unity and single-mindedness amongst the Jews that cannot be surpassed by any other widely dispersed ethnic group of its dimensions. **They call** themselves the chosen, the first born of god, and relegate the rest of the world to one heap, called the *goyim*, the gentiles i.e. those *lower grade humans* that they, the Jews, are destined to rule, at god's behest.

As I have previously noted in this book, and the other books that I have written on the subject of astrotheology, **the actual function** of the seven Jewish feasts is to track the movements of the sun throughout the solar year. **The purpose** of the feasts is to mark the positions of the sun as it crosses certain coordinates that indicate the changing of the seasons, harvesting, planting, or other agricultural and/or mundane activities. **The Fall festivals** of *Rosh Hashanah*, *Yom Kippur*, and *Sukkoth* mark the passage of the sun into the netherworld, that is, the cosmic region below the equinoxes, as well as having clear agricultural significances.

The trend of the environment on earth is determined by the seasons, and **it is the sun** that dictates the seasons - this was quite evident to the primitives of ancient times; hence the ancients positioned festivals at dates in their calendars that tagged the major transitional points or passages of the sun. **Transitional points of the sun** are, of course, the **cardinal points**. Within forty days of the sun passing through a cosmic transitional point or cardinal point if you will, the earth's environment changes, for good or bad, in response to the indicated movements of the sun.

The cardinal points are the Vernal Equinox, Summer Solstice, Autumnal Equinox, and the Winter Solstice. The equinoxes mark the transits of the sun between the upper and lower hemispheres; and the solstices mark the

Section One

The Secret Origins Of Judaism

beginnings of either summer or winter. So whenever the sun approached or reached one of the cardinal points, it served as an **indicator** to the earth's inhabitants of environmental **transitions** soon to follow.

The *tenor* and *mood* of the various festivals were patterned so as to reflect the anticipated climatic changes, whether good or bad. The fall of the sun below the equinox, marked by Yom Kippur, is an *indicator* of a coming *oppressive earthly environment* - the winter season; hence the *tenor* and *tone* of the Yom Kippur festival was geared in *dreaded anticipation* of the **perils** of the winter months. **At this time of dread,** the ancient primitives were *penitent*, they sought god's mercy and forgiveness, his aid and guidance. They engaged in self flagellation, fasting; they made blood sacrifices to the good spirits and the bad spirits - as noted in the Jewish custom of sacrificing not only to Yahweh but to Azazel also, the demon of the wilderness or abyss. **These customs all spring from** an ancient primordial, animistic past, wherein the primitives believed that the forces of nature were controlled and manipulated by unseen spirits and demons, and that those unseen spirits and demons could be influenced by prayer, sacrifices, gifts, and entreaties.

In the original **primitive origins** of the self-flagellation rituals, self denial, penitence, etc, Yom Kippur, indeed, represents penitence, but also a preemptive punishment of self for one's sins, an assault on one's self - self flagellation.

At the point of the sun's descent into the underworld, the ancients sought to appease god with **self affliction** so as to lessen the annual seasonal afflictions of the winter season, which, in those early primordial times, they attributed to the god's chastisement or chastening by reason of their errors or sins, rather than to natural seasonal cycles....*Leviticus 16:29-31 And this <u>shall be a statute for ever unto you</u>: that in the <u>seventh month, on the tenth day of the month</u>, ye shall **afflict** your souls, and do no work at all, whether it be one of your own country, or a stranger that sojourneth among you: For on that day shall the priest make an atonement for you, to cleanse you, that ye may be clean from all your sins before the LORD. It shall be a sabbath of rest unto you, and **ye shall afflict your souls**, by a statute for ever.*

Section One

The Secret Origins Of Judaism

The *rituals* of the festivals of each era reflect that *particular* era, also traditions carried forward; but the cultural-religious modifications **will be distinct** to the period, influences, and region. **Hence our festivals are periodically re-created** in keeping with the cultural and intellectual evolution of the populace. **As the societies evolve** *spiritually* and *intellectually*, **they infuse** the elements of their *enlightenment* or evolved ideas into the definitions or explanations of their religious and **cultural customs.** Thus people's religious traditions, in terms of the meanings given for them, are altered, modified, or *refocused* in keeping with the exigencies of the cultural era - such is the case with Judaism.

All of the ancient Jewish festivals began as nature, seasonal, and agricultural rites - no divine revelations or direct and provable godly input was involved in the development of Jewish culture. **The Jewish culture evolved** or developed its modern day religious content over many hundreds of years of societal evolution. Judaism did not burst upon the cultural scene ready-made and a finished product.

We know that Judaism evolved and modified itself significantly from about the 6th century B.C. to about the 2nd century B.C.; and then again from about the 2nd century B.C. to about A.D. 200, and then again from about the 3rd century A.D. *in stages*, to our present era under the influences of powerful and influential Rabbinic sects.

Our comparisons of Rabbinic Judaism to Biblical Judaism leave no doubt that *Judaism has transformed and recreated itself* significantly over the centuries. History shows that society hardly ever jettisons its old ancient traditions completely, excepting those of the most barbarous type; rather they find ways to adapt their old customs to their evolving cultures by adding **new interpretations to the old traditions.**

The Jewish religion started as a local tribal cult, centered around a imaginary *ethereal god-king* housed within a local shrine; ritualistically served and worshipped through bizarre primitive ceremonies and sacrificial bloodletting. **This is the message** that I have derived for myself, rationally, from an evaluation of the biblical passages that we have examined. **I do not**

Section One

The Secret Origins Of Judaism

understand how any rational person, if dominated by reason, can argue against the *facts* of our presentation. **However**, it is easily understood how some beleaguered souls, who may have spent most of their lives *sincerely committed* to a religious farce, are apprehensively reluctant, and indeed fearful, of admitting, at this decisive juncture in their lives, of momentous spiritual portent, that, in fact, **they have been duped**. There can be no reasonable or rational doubt of this reality: that the assertions of the Jews, as to divine sponsorship, collapse totally when placed under the weight of prudent analyses.

Eventually, at some point, the monotheists must face the facts as they really are - they must cross the Rubicon; thereby acknowledging and accepting as undeniable fact, that they, regrettably, are the unfortunate victims of the vilest and the cruelest of all deceptions... Spiritual Wickedness. To quote from my book, *The Biggest Lie Ever Told, 4th Edition*: "If any part of the scriptures are open to question as to whether it is fable or literal, than the complete scriptures must, by all rules of common sense, be subject to the same critique...These are facts that we must deal with rationally and dispassionately if we sincerely want to find the truth".

Sukkoth

Now, we arrive at **Sukkoth**, the seventh and last of the Seven Jewish Feast. Sukkoth closes out the year of feasts. Sukkoth extends initially for seven days, from the Full Moon of Tishri 15 to Tishri 22; but two additional ceremonial days have been added which takes the full term of events to nine days. **Shemini Atzeret** is observed on the eighth day, and **Simchat Torah** is normally observed on the ninth and final day of the Sukkoth festivities.

Sukkoth is one of the three so-called *Pilgrim Feasts* - the others are **Pesach** (Passover) and **Shavuot** (Feast of Weeks). These were feasts whereas in olden times, when the Temple of Solomon *allegedly* stood in Jerusalem, all of the Jews were called to make pilgrimage to Jerusalem for a grand assembly before Yahweh at his Temple. They were not to come empty handed, but rather with contributions of assets for the Temple

Section One

The Secret Origins Of Judaism

god.......*Deuteronomy 16:16-17* <u>*Three times in a year shall all thy males appear before the LORD*</u> *thy god in the place which he shall choose; in the feast of unleavened bread, and in the feast of weeks, and in the feast of tabernacles:* <u>*and they shall not appear before the LORD empty:*</u> *Every man shall give as he is able, according to the blessing of the LORD thy god which he hath given thee.......*It seems that the ancient gods were similar to the modern gods - they all desire money.

Sukkoth is often called the fruit harvest because it was in the autumn that the bumper crops of grapes and apples and such were harvested. You may have noticed that in various ancient cultures, the autumn harvest was a time of great revelry, gaiety, licentiousness, and so forth as typified by the Roman festival of Bacchanalia. **One of the reasons** for the revelry of the Fall season was the custom of converting portions of the fruit harvest to spirits, that is, alcoholic spirits, wine and whatever. Also there was an ancient animistic belief or superstition that the evil demons of darkness *or* the *coming new year* could be frightened away by loud clamorous noises and banging and so forth, such as we yet do in greeting our modern New Years.

The term Sukkoth translates to Booths - the Jews allege that the Booths of Sukkoth are types of the temporary dwellings that they (their ancestors) were forced to live in following their godly emancipation from bondage in Egypt. As the story goes, they departed Egypt in great haste, and subsequently wandered about in the desert for forty long years, and were forced to shelter themselves in temporary dwellings by reason of these circumstances. They suffered and endured forty long years of trials and tribulations, wandering from place to place until Yahweh finally delivered or directed them toward the promised land of the covenant.

So Yahweh commanded, according to the bible, that the Hebrews forever hold in remembrance god's grace and favor toward them by the institution of the sacred festival of Sukkoth, from generation to generation in perpetuity, commencing each year on the fifteenth day of the seventh month i.e. Tishri 15. **By god's instruction, as stipulated by the bible,** the Jews are commanded to gather twigs, greenery, branches and the like, and to

Section One

The Secret Origins Of Judaism

construct single room huts or booths which they are to dwell in for seven full days in remembrance of the sufferings of their ancestors, and the benevolence of their savior god, Yahweh.

The rectangular booths are constructed with three walls and one open side. **The walls** are constructed of whatever material that's available, whether tarps, sheets, planks, metal, or what have you; **but the roofs** of the booths must be overlaid or constructed with the *greenery, boughs, branches* and such as characterized by the biblical instructions - **see the following** where god speaks in the *first person*:

Biblical command for Sukkoth........Leviticus 23:39-44 Also in the fifteenth day of the seventh month, when ye have gathered in the fruit of the land, ye shall keep a feast unto the LORD seven days: on the first day shall be a sabbath, and on the eighth day shall be a sabbath. And **ye shall** take you on the first day the boughs of goodly trees, branches of palm trees, and the boughs of thick trees, and willows of the brook; and **ye shall** rejoice before the LORD your god seven days. And **ye shall** keep it a feast unto the LORD seven days in the year. It shall be a statute for ever in your generations: **ye shall** celebrate it in the seventh month. **Ye shall** dwell in booths seven days; all that are Israelites born shall dwell in booths: That your generations may know that **I made** the children of Israel to dwell in booths, when **I brought them out** of the land of Egypt: **I am the LORD your god.** And Moses declared unto the children of Israel the feasts of the LORD.

Also take note of these verses: Nehemiah 8:14-18 And they found written in the law which the LORD had commanded by Moses, that the children of Israel should dwell in booths in the feast of the seventh month: And that they should publish and proclaim in all their cities, and in Jerusalem, saying, Go forth unto the mount, and fetch olive branches, and pine branches, and myrtle branches, and palm branches, and branches of thick trees, to make booths, as it is written. So the people went forth, and brought them, and made themselves booths, every one upon the roof of his house, and in their courts, and in the courts of the house of god, and in the street of the water gate, and in the street of the gate of Ephraim. And all the congregation of

Section One

The Secret Origins Of Judaism

them that were come again out of the captivity made booths, and sat under the booths: for since the days of Jeshua the son of Nun unto that day had not the children of Israel done so. And there was very great gladness. Also day by day, from the first day unto the last day, he read in the book of the law of god. And they kept the feast seven days; and on the eighth day was a solemn assembly, according unto the manner.

As noted above, the Sukkoth festival, in its entirety, extends for nine days - the first seven days carry traditional Sukkoth ceremonies centered around the daily occupancies of the Booths. There are many prayers, rituals, sacrifices, and Torah/Bible readings that are conducted during the seven days of the Sukkoth ceremonies but we need not delineate them within this essay - **our focus must remain** on the big picture, which is the *true significance* of the Jewish tradition requiring the *building of shanty huts* as an obligation to god.

The eighth day of Shemini Atzeret is billed as a day of assembly, whereas the Jewish community gathers together in solemn ceremony for the occasion. **The ninth day of Simchat Torah**, which means *rejoicing in the Torah*, is centered around the traditional readings of portions of the Torah, with special regards to the **closing** of the year, and the **beginning** of the New Year.

The Jews claim that the Sukkoth traditions are in remembrance of god's beneficence, and the covenantal obligations of the Jewish people, as noted above. They, the Jews, find spiritual significance in remembering a time when they had nothing as individuals nor as a nation - not even reliable shelters; but rather were homeless, camped out in the wilderness, with only rickety booths held together by scrap twigs, branches, and other assorted available materials, that gave them but temporary cover from the elements. But through all this they held faith in their god of deliverance, **Yahweh**, who in time, blessed and elevated them.

So even though they may now live in wealth and plenty, with abundant resources that far exceed their needs, it behooves them to recall the times of their nation's past when they were homeless vagabonds with only their god

Section One

The Secret Origins Of Judaism

as a friend. They are called forth by their clergy to forever keep their duties and obligations to god in the forefront of their hopes and ambitions, and *above all* never to fall from their sacred contract with Yahweh - that indeed, they are wedded to god by a divine covenant, unlike and above all others. They are the chosen and the destined of god, and the seven Jewish feasts, are sanctioned as reminders of their covenant and specialness.

The virtuous aspirations referenced above are very laudable, and I truly applaud the vaunted ethical, spiritual aspects of Judaism - I truly do. But in regards to the *festival traditions of the Jews*, which in explaining, they have **lavishly garnished** with pious, noble, and sublime religious connotations; I must earnestly submit and declare, that this *sentimental facade*, in truth, smacks of a fraudulent religious **veneer** painted over a *pagan heathen core*. I think that the *facts in evidence* that we have presented thus far in this essay give unassailable credence and support to this allegation, which I regret having to make, but make it we must, in the superior interest of truth.

As to the *true* origins of the Sukkoth Feast, and the building of the shanties that the Jews claim served as temporary shelters during their sojourns and wanderings in the wilderness; the Jews never wandered about in the desert for forty years, and hence they never built Booths as temporary shelters under the circumstances that they assert. Secular history has no records of a Hebrew enslavement in Egypt, as depicted in the bible, and it follows that the exodus from Egypt and the wanderings in the desert likewise are not historical.

Sukkoth originated as an agricultural festival amongst the ancient Semites and others, a harvest festival. **Temporary shelters are essential** and integral to mass, broad based harvesting, processing, and stowing of crops. This was so anciently and the same applies in modern times - **even today** *migrant pickers* live in temporary housing supplied by the farmers that they work for. End of the year harvesting was not a casual affair anciently - it was a community effort, which is a reason why Sukkoth was tagged as a pilgrim festival in the bible, that required the Hebrews from near and far to gather at the sight of harvesting.

Section One

The Secret Origins Of Judaism

The harvesting had to be completed within time constraints that avoided the loss of crops due to rot, rain, or other hazards. There was a window of limited time between the ripeness of the crop and over-ripeness wherein the harvesting had to be done; *plus* the crops had to be processed *and* preserved for future use throughout the coming months. The pilgrims that traveled to the Jerusalem area, or wherever, to aid in the community effort of harvesting needed temporary shelter for the extended days and weeks of harvesting and processing; consequently they built lean-to huts (Booths) and the like from the scraps, shrubs, branches, boughs, and such that were at hand.

The original Sukkoth festival, under whatever name, was an agricultural festival or tradition with no religious significance whatsoever - that developed or was generated naturally among the ancients, resultant from the mass influx of peasants gathered or ingathered at the times of harvesting. **As the Jewish religion developed** amongst the Semites they sought to change the various agricultural holidays of the year, including Sukkoth, into religious holidays, by inventing new religious meanings or reasons for the seasonal assemblies. **The Rabbis constructed this absurd yarn** about the suffering wandering Jews living in Booths so as to give a *religious veneer* to an old heathen agricultural festival.

This completes our review of the *Seven Jewish Feasts*. The Jews claim that these feasts are integral to their covenant with god - a covenant which sets the Jewish race or tribe as god's vicegerents here on earth. Judaism is the foundation of modern monotheism. Judaism, Christianity, and Islam *share*, to a significant degree, *the same prophets*; from Adam to Elijah, and the hosts of prophets in between. In light of the *persuasive* information that we have presented in this essay as to the true pagan origins of biblical Judaism - from primitive nature and sacrificial rites, I think that many of us may feel faced with an unwelcomed dilemma; which is this: how do we hold onto our traditional faith but yet reject the heinous and absurd practices and assertions within the Torah, Bible and Quran.

In many parts of the bible, *god speaks in the first person*, commanding us to perform ludicrous primitive pagan sacrificial rites, burnings and

Section One

The Secret Origins Of Judaism

bloodlettings. **We are commanded** by god, according to the bible, to slaughter certain animals, and splatter the blood of these sacrificial animals about or upon the walls, altars, shrines, buildings, and such as a means of communicating our devotion to god. We have quoted some of these verses within this book; *so how*, by what trick of the mind's cognitive processes shall we *excuse* these absurdities, *and continue* proclaiming to the world that our god, that is to say the god of Abraham, the god of monotheism is the only true god. **Shall we reject** parts of the scriptures but nevertheless revere other portions, and yet proclaim that the scriptures are holy, or perhaps semi-holy? Or, **shall we face the facts** as they truly are, admit that we have been the unwitting victims of a vile and cruel deception, and thereafter somehow muster the courage and strength to *reexamine* and *reevaluate* our inherited traditions?

I submit for your perusal a quotation from my previous book, Lifting The Gnostic Veil:..."*We need to understand clearly our options when trying to access the origins of our religious creeds – they have either sprung from the mouth of god or the mind of man. These are our only two options, and if the latter holds true, which it does, that our religious traditions originated from our own expansive imaginations, then the course to their (our religious traditions) correct evaluation is relatively simple: we need only to trace and decipher our cultural history. The correct answers to all of our religious questions, relative to the generation of the various religious creeds that we revere, lies in the records of history; but the major problem that confronts us is the monumental task of separating myth from actual history, and then accurately interpreting both the chronicles of past historical ages and the ubiquitous fables penned as historical events. Our religious ideas and concepts have been generated by our minds' interactions with our environments, our cultures, and our experiences*".

I think that the quote from my previous book is on target. The major question that confronts us in our efforts to find truth is this: by what methods shall we determine the legitimacy or illegitimacy of our religious credos. **Shall we seek** to reinforce our *faith* through prayer, scriptural readings, and such, with high hopes that god will somehow bless us with

Section One

The Secret Origins Of Judaism

spiritual clarity and insight; or, on the other hand, **shall we dare** to incorporate the underutilized assets of logic, reason, intellect, and courage. Will we muster the courage to accept the verdicts of truth, whether or not such verdicts are welcomed and comforting or sadly, disheartening. **Our investigation** has presented a preponderance of evidence that *Judaism is a man-made concoction*, completely devoid of godly sponsorship. This verdict is certain when the historical evidence is viewed and analyzed dispassionately.

There can be no rational doubt in the verdict. **There is compelling evidence** that all of the world's religions have sprung from the wells of Man's imaginations. Judaism, and, in effect, monotheism in total cannot be excluded from this verdict. The only way for the religionists to appeal or overturn our verdict is to present historical and/or rational proofs of godly sponsorship. But when it comes to religion, the religionists are only capable of appealing to our emotions and faith - they lack a cogent argument that can positively or favorably influence our reason and intellect.

For certain, they shout that the world must have a god, there must be a creator! However, even if we admit the existence of a Creator god, such an admission does not, in any way, transfer legitimacy to the Judaic, Christian, and Muslim doctrines. **A verifiable connection between the Creator and Jewish monotheism does not exist!** The reasoning of some monotheists is so parochial that they think that there are *only two options* as to god's existence, that is, either their sectarian god is the Creator and lord or there is no god at all. They seemingly fail to realize or understand, or choose to ignore, that the history of the world shows gods aplenty.

The fact is, our creator is *unknown*; and not only is god unknown, but he is also unknowable, according to the Ancients. The idea of reducing god to the configuration of a ghostly humanoid is very primitive. It may be that a better pathway to god is through self-introspection, the sciences; and by way of avenues that connect and blend us with the *Mind of god* - rather than through emotional wailings and/or concocted fairytales. **All religions have**

Section One

The Secret Origins Of Judaism

originated, as verified by the records of secular history, **from Man's imagination**, as shaped and influenced by environment and culture.

Imagination, itself, is not a bad thing; it is, perhaps, the greatest spiritual gift of all in my opinion, because imagination breaks the boundaries of thought. Imagination allows us to *image* things or *bring form* to things (ideas) outside of our experiences, and to excel beyond the limitations of the five senses. Imagination allows us to conceptualize and hypothesize beyond the limitations of space and time. However, our imaginations of the *unknown worlds* are usually constrained, limited, or configured in reflection of our language, and associations within the known world, that which is tangible, mundane, and familiar.

In consequence, the conceptualized gods and demons of ancient times, which in fact were created out of Man's imaginations, show clear correlations to the prevailing cultures of those times. When Man pictured god as a natural force or, later in time, as a monarch or king with a heavenly court, this shows Man fashioning god, the unknown quality, in reflection of his comprehension or conception of the known quality (world and culture) in which he was resident. Logic readily reveals why nomadic shepherds, watching their sheep at night, would imagine their god as a *heavenly shepherd* - 'twas simply a mirrored reflection of their perceptions of themselves and their environment. They *worded* their conceptions of the unknown spiritual world in the language or vernacular of the known earthly world.

Section One

The Secret Origins Of Judaism

Section Two: Evolution Of The Sabbath

Although not officially termed a feast, The *Saturday* Sabbath is most prominent amongst Jewish holy days. In the 23rd chapter of Leviticus of the bible, **the Saturday Sabbath is ranked first before all other feasts**, wherein god instructs Moses on the requirements of the Seven Jewish Feasts or Holy Convocations. **The Seven Feasts** are also **Sabbaths**. The bible stipulates that the Sabbath must be strictly observed by the Jewish people, and threatens severe punishment if the Jews fail to follow the demands of the weekly Sabbath. It is part of the divine covenant between the Jewish people and Yahweh that the Sabbaths be kept in perpetuity.... *Leviticus 23:1-4 And the LORD spake unto Moses, saying, Speak unto the children of Israel, and say unto them, Concerning the feasts of the LORD, which ye shall proclaim to be holy convocations, even **these are my feasts**. Six days shall work be done: but the seventh day is the sabbath of rest, an holy convocation;* ye shall do no work therein: *it is the sabbath of the LORD in all your dwellings.* **These are the feasts of the LORD**, *even holy convocations, which ye shall proclaim in their seasons*.

In fact all of the seven Jewish feasts are also Sabbaths, meaning more or less that these days are sanctified, special days, that are owed, dedicated, or promised to god by reason of the Jewish covenant with god. According to the bible, God, himself, established the Sabbath, and made it obligatory that the Jews observe the Sabbath. The Sabbath is the *seventh day* of the week, and it (the 7th day) is designated as a sanctified day in Genesis of the bible. As the story goes, god created the world in six days, and rested from his labors on the seventh day, and that is why we have the seven day week - so as to mimic the pattern of god who worked six days at creating the universe and then rested on the seventh day....*Genesis 2:2-3 And on the seventh day god ended his work which he had made; and he rested on the seventh day from all his work which he had made. And god blessed the seventh day, and sanctified it: because that in it he had rested from all his work which god created and made....Exodus 31:16-17 Wherefore the children of Israel shall keep the sabbath, to observe the sabbath throughout their generations, for a perpetual covenant.* It is a

The Secret Origins Of Judaism

sign between me and the children of Israel for ever: for in six days the LORD made heaven and earth, and on the seventh day he rested, and was refreshed.

As mentioned above **the observance of the Sabbath is required** - it is not optional. Working is disallowed on the Sabbath. There are several prohibitions attached to the Sabbath - *not working* is but one of the provisions. By god's decree, there are severe penalties awaiting those that violate the Sabbath - even death. Take note of the following verses wherein the Jewish *god ordered the execution* of an individual for gathering some firewood or such on the Sabbath - gathering wood on the Sabbath, you see, is a form of prohibited work according to Judaic biblical doctrine....*Numbers 15:32-36 And while the children of Israel were in the wilderness, they found a <u>man that gathered sticks upon the sabbath day</u>. And they that found him gathering sticks brought him unto Moses and Aaron, and unto all the congregation. And they put him in ward, because it was not declared what should be done to him. <u>And the LORD said</u> unto Moses, The man shall be surely put to death: all the congregation shall stone him with stones without the camp. And all the congregation brought him without the camp, and stoned him with stones, and he died; <u>as the LORD commanded Moses</u>.*

The death sentence demanded by god in the verses above is not an isolated instance, there are several verses in the bible wherein god reiterates that death is the punishment for violating the Sabbath. **Think of what we just read** in the biblical verses above - god instructed Moses to **kill** a man for gathering sticks on the Sabbath. This declaration comes from a book that stands as the foundation for all monotheistic belief. Witness the following biblical quotes concerning god's law and punishments for violations of the Sabbaths:........*Exodus 31:14 Ye shall keep the sabbath therefore; for it is holy unto you: <u>every one that defileth it shall surely be put to death</u>: for whosoever doeth any work therein, that soul shall be cut off from among his people........Exodus 35:2 Six days shall work be done, but on the seventh day there shall be to you an holy day, a sabbath of rest to the LORD: <u>whosoever doeth work therein shall be put to death</u>.*

The prohibitions of the Jewish Sabbath are wide-ranging, ludicrous, petty, and mystifying. In compliance with biblical and Rabbinical Judaism, the Jews are not allowed to turn on lights on the Sabbath. They are not

Section Two

The Secret Origins Of Judaism

allowed to cook and bake. They are not allowed to light a fire or carry items beyond a certain distance from their domain. They are not allowed to work or farm. They are not allowed to conduct business, or buy and sell. They are not allowed to ride in conveyances, or travel but short distances from their domain, if allowed to travel at all. There are myriad petty things that they *are not allowed* to do, to numerous for me to note here without boring you to death; such as grass mowing, laundry, writing, cutting, using the computer or telephone, or shopping - **the restrictions go on and on**.

All Jews, of course, are not endowed with equal amounts of religious zeal; and consequently they are not, as a community, in total agreement on which prohibitions must be followed and obeyed, out of the seemingly countless restrictions. There are, *at least*, three well-known religious categories of Jews, that is the Orthodox, Reform, and Conservative. They differ *as groups* as to the particulars of the Sabbath. I'm sure that they also differ *as individuals* as to what extent they are willing to conform to the Sabbath rules. **But the puzzling enigma** that you and I are faced with is that this proclamation *of Death to all violators of the Sabbath* is even found in the bible - and moreover, cited as coming directly from the mouth of god. **So whether people are presently being killed** for violating the Sabbath or not is not the point - that such a heinous directive is attributed to god within god's book, the bible, is the issue that should give us great pause.

It is important that we understand that all of the Jewish feasts are, in fact, Sabbaths, that is to say, they are special days set aside for performing certain rituals in reverence to the Jewish god. The term Sabbath is not restricted to the Saturday Sabbath. Our word Sabbath is the translation of the Jewish **Shabbat** which means to cease or to rest. Of course the bible gives the impression that the *day of rest* was implemented in semblance of god's repose at the conclusion of his creation activities - the bible states that god was refreshed by his resting on the seventh day. This implication of god resting because he was weary *is a diversion*, a silly diversion at that - can you really imagine the Creator god of the universe needing a day to rest, to relax or get some shut-eye so to speak.

Section Two

The Secret Origins Of Judaism

The actual *functional* meaning of *Sabbath* or *Shabbat* as a day of *rest* or *cessation* is to culminate, that is the culmination of a cycle; or the *marking* of a period of time, or duration as a *pivotal point* or *turning point*. The Jewish calendar is a lunar based *mathematical formula* or system for measuring the year with 7 as the *operative number*. The 7 is oft repeated within the Jewish calendar system, from 7 days, 7 weeks (Feast of Weeks), 7 Months (Feasts), 7 Years (Fallow year), 7 leap years to the Metonic Cycle, and the 7 times 7 completed to the Jubilee Year. The Jewish *lunar* calendar revolves around the Moon and the number 7. The Shabbat or Seven (7), that is to say, the Sabbath as a *day of rest* or *cessation* merely indicates the *point of renewal* of the cycle of 7. Likewise when the Sabbath is appointed to a feast, it marks the feast as a point of rest or cessation which simply means, in regards to the functionalism, a point at which a cycle, *of whatever term*, is **culminated, renewed or commenced**.

Also, it is very important to note, that in some cases a *Sabbath* is used as a *place setter*, as, for example, with the Egyptians who created a mathematical calendar year of 360 days. **In order** to keep their calendar in sync with the sun, the Egyptians appended five (5) Sabbath (epagomenal) days to the end of each year as *blank place setters* or *uncounted days* that took the actual year to the correct term of 365 days. The Egyptians used a 360-day year in order to facilitate mathematical computations of larger cycles from a base of 360 days, which *corresponds to 360 degrees*. All cycles (circles, ellipses, rotations, revolutions) are measured at 360 degrees, so by reducing their annual day-count to 360 days, they, the Egyptians, facilitated their cosmic math and also provided certain numerical correlations from cycle to cycle. I covered this issue of parallel cycles in *Book Four of The Astrological Foundation Of The Christ Myth*.

A Sabbath, *in terms of its calendrical functions*, **is a Sabbath** (place setter, indicator, pivot) regardless of whatever name we may call it. **The Jews used the term** *Shabbat* - some other cultures may have accomplished the *same Sabbath function* under another name. For instance, nowadays, at each Leap Year, we add an extra day to the Gregorian calendar, that is to say, a special day, a type of Sabbath, a dedicated day whose *function* is to add another day

Section Two

The Secret Origins Of Judaism

as a *place setter* (29th of February) to the calendar so as to keep the calendar in sync with the solar annual cycle. The Jewish Sabbath was a *functional* unit (place setter, indicator, pivot) by which the Jews adjusted their calendar and/or marked certain points in their calendar - **it was not** *just* a Saturday observance. **As an example**, if you wanted to use a year of *thirteen months* at *twenty-eight days* to the month, the total days would amount to 364 days, one short of a solar year. So by adding a Sabbath day, under whatever name, to the end of the year, a culture could thereby keep their calendar in sync with the annual sun cycle.

As a reminder, I should mention, at this juncture, that our purpose within this essay is to trace all of the Jewish feasts, including the Sabbath and the other Seven Feasts, to their *pre-religious functions*. **The modern explanations** that the Jews give us for the Sabbath rituals, whether the Saturday Sabbaths or the seven Feasts, **are made-up or concocted** religious interpretations that obscure the true primitive *non-religious or calendrical* functions of the Jewish Sabbaths. We have already uncovered the primitive, pagan origins of the seven traditional Jewish feasts, now it remains for us to uncover the true origin of the *Saturday* Sabbath tradition.

The explanation given by the Jews for the Saturday Sabbath is very, very bizarre. The Jewish congregations are told that the Sabbath follows a pattern set by god, of resting on the 7th day - this is followed by the **biblical threat to kill** anyone who chooses *not* to rest. I think that it's abundantly clear, or should be, that there must be more to the *Shabbat* than we have been told, because certainly the given explanation is **not rational**.

The bible informs us that the *Feast days*, the *New Moons*, and the *Full moons* likewise, were all Sabbaths. In other words, in keeping with the definitions that I have supplied above, these *markers* on the calendar, and *phases of the moon* were *indicators* of the duration, beginning, pausing, and renewal of cycles. **Please review** the following biblical verses wherein the Sabbaths are equated with the feasts and the lunar cycles. Within these verses, you will notice that *fallowing,* that is to say, the temporary cessation of planting and harvesting the land *is called a Sabbath,* that the New Moons

Section Two

The Secret Origins Of Judaism

are Sabbaths, that the Appointed Feasts are Sabbaths and so on.......**The Seventh Year is called a Sabbath**: *Leviticus 25:4 But in the seventh year shall be a <u>sabbath of rest unto the land</u>, a sabbath for the LORD: thou shalt neither sow thy field, nor prune thy vineyard*.......**The Jubilee is called a Sabbath**: *Leviticus 25:8-10 And thou shalt number <u>seven sabbaths of years</u> unto thee, seven times seven years; and the space of the seven sabbaths of years shall be unto thee forty and nine years. Then shalt thou cause the trumpet of the jubile to sound on the tenth day of the seventh month, in the day of atonement shall ye make the trumpet sound throughout all your land. <u>And ye shall hallow the fiftieth year</u>, and proclaim liberty throughout all the land unto all the inhabitants thereof: it shall be a jubile unto you; and ye shall return every man unto his possession, and ye shall return every man unto his family*.......**The Feast of Atonement is called a Sabbath**: *Leviticus 16:29-31 And this shall be a statute for ever unto you: that in the seventh month, on the tenth day of the month, ye shall afflict your souls, and do no work at all, whether it be one of your own country, or a stranger that sojourneth among you: For on that day shall the priest make an atonement for you, to cleanse you, that ye may be clean from all your sins before the LORD. <u>It shall be a sabbath of rest unto you</u>, and ye shall afflict your souls, by a statute for ever*.......**The Feast of Sukkoth (Tabernacles) is called a Sabbath**: *Leviticus 23:39 Also in the fifteenth day of the seventh month, when ye have gathered in the fruit of the land, ye shall keep a feast unto the LORD seven days: <u>on the first day</u> <u>shall be a sabbath, and on the eighth day</u> <u>shall be a sabbath</u>*.

It is fundamentally important that we understand that the term *Sabbath* or *Shabbat* is *not restricted* to the *Saturday* Sabbath, but rather that various especially noted dates on the ancient Jewish calendar were designated as **Sabbaths**. These dates were called Shabbat (or <u>Shabattu</u> by some others) *because of their functions* - functions that gave a specific designation to the date in question. **This system** of assigning Sabbath (Shabbat) designations to particular days was prevalent amongst the ancient Babylonians, and some other Semitic tribes, and among the non-Semitic Sumerians before them all. It is agreed that the Sumerians originated the system, which was later assimilated by the Semites on coming into contact with Sumerian culture. **The Jews copied and modified the system**, primarily, from the Babylonians. We shall explore the seminal connections between Babylonian culture and Jewish culture shortly.

Section Two

The Secret Origins Of Judaism

The **Jewish calendar and festivals have been derived from the ancient Sumerians of Mesopotamia**. The Sumerians were not Semitic people - it is said by some historians that they were of the same stock as the ancient Egyptians. A confederacy or various groups of Semitic tribes made inroads into ancient Sumer circa 3000 B.C., and continued expanding their domination over the unfolding centuries. **These prehistoric Semites were nomadic warlike tribes** believed to have migrated out of the Arabian Peninsula - **they were**, according to historians, **barbarians** and did not possess a written language.

The **Sumerians, who as before noted were *Non*-Semitic, were a highly civilized people** with a great civilization stretching along the fertile, verdant lands of the Tigris and Euphrates rivers. **Waves of invading Semites,** from which the Semitic Jews and Semitic Arabs are descended, poured out from the barren deserts of Arabia, and over time **overcame the Sumerians**, and, in conquest, seized or **adopted their culture**, alphabet, systems and mythologies. Eventually the Semites **established** the much acclaimed **Empire** of *Akkad and Sumer.*

At the <u>core</u> of the Sumerian culture was their <u>*Church Calendar*</u>, as so aptly described by *Stephen Langdon* in his book *Babylonian Menologies and the Semitic Calendars.* **The ancient Sumerian calendar was a lunar-solar calendar** of 12 months with a 13th month inserted at intervals so as to keep the calendar in tune with the seasons. **Each month of the Sumerian calendar had its own mythology** reflective of the stars and constellations that accompanied each month in succession.

The calendar of ancient Nippur of Sumer, that is **the Sumerian calendar, was <u>saturated</u> with religious festivals** that marked the sacred or special days of each month; they had special days marked as *unlucky*, or *lucky*, or *sacred*, and days on which various activities were either allowed or prohibited. **The Sumerians**, had viewed and studied the heliacal risings that greeted each new month and, in consequence, **had recorded mythological tales** in association with those cosmic lights. The menologies of each month also described the activities associated with the month such as planting,

Section Two

The Secret Origins Of Judaism

harvesting, irrigation, migration, building, what have you. **Indeed, the template by which the Jews have constructed their** *calendar of the covenant* **was bequeathed to them by the ancient sages of Sumer**, as evidence indicates - by way of the Semitic Babylonians, and not by their fictitious god.

Babylonian Origin Of The Jewish Sabbath

At this point in our investigation, I'm sure that we are all thoroughly convinced that the popular Jewish declaration of divine sponsorship for their religion and tribe is totally without merit; in fact, based on the evidence at hand, the claim is absolutely ludicrous. We have shown that the seven Jewish feasts are palpably devoid of any *divine* seminal connection - **all that remains is to trace the Sabbath** rituals to their pagan, or perhaps we should say, *primitive* origins.

Our major concern within this section is to explore from whence the Sabbath (Shabbat) traditions are truly derived. **We want to know the source** of the queer, bizarre rituals embodied in the Shabbat traditions. **What is the true origin**, and is there a logical explanation for the odd goings-on inherent within the Jewish Shabbat. **We don't accept**, for a minute, that god almighty is the founder of the Sabbath i.e. Shabbat tradition. The peculiar Jewish Shabbat rituals do not, in any way, reflect the intelligence that we *rationals* normally associate with **the concept of god**.

The historical connection between the Jews and ancient Mesopotamia is not hidden. **The bible states** that the first patriarch of the Jews, Abraham (Abram), came from **Ur**, which was a city of ancient Mesopotamia.......*Genesis 11:31 And Terah took Abram his son, and Lot the son of Haran his son's son, and Sarai his daughter in law, his son Abram's wife; and they went forth with them from Ur of the Chaldees, to go into the land of Canaan; and they came unto Haran, and dwelt there....***Likewise**, we know that **Babylon** was also a locale of ancient Mesopotamia. So even without the inclusion of the famous Babylonian Exile of the Jews pegged at B.C. 586, we find a prior

Section Two

The Secret Origins Of Judaism

historical affinity between Jewish Culture and Mesopotamian culture, of which Babylon was a major component. **The Jews have assimilated, adapted, and modified Babylonian culture and traditions, and made it their own** - this assertion is absolutely incontrovertible, based on our comparisons of Babylonian and Judaic traditions. Judaic Semitic culture is the child of Mesopotamian Semitic culture, and in particular Babylonian culture. The traditions of Judaism are not traditions bestowed by god, but rather are *Semitic traditions inherited from their ancient forbears* that they, the Jews, have fraudulently and impiously labeled as commandments from god.

All religions have a cultural root - it can be no other way, unless the claims of godly revelations to certain individuals are actually true - and this, most certainly, cannot be so. **The assertions** made by the clergies that the Creator (god) of the entire universe actually reveals himself to certain chosen individuals from time to time, and that in turn, these chosen individuals share god's message with the rest of us, is not even worth intelligent consideration, to my way of thinking. This leaves only the Mind of Man, the **fertile imagination** inherent in all of us, as the true fashioner of our various religious doctrines.

All religions have evolved through our cultures, and the path to the true and verifiable origins of our religious beliefs or doctrines is through a *dispassionate* examination of religion in the context of a *cultural* component. **This is the path** that we are now pursuing, in our effort, to attain the true origins of Judaism. **The roots** of Judaism are found chiefly, even if not entirely, in the folds of ancient Semitic and Sumerian culture. This is the **focus** of our **inquiry**, as we continue.

Section Two

The Secret Origins Of Judaism

Let us begin our comparisons between the Judaic and Babylonian cultures by viewing their calendar months. One need not be a philologist or etymologist to notice the glaring relationships between the Babylonian names for the months and the Jewish names. **The similarities** in the calendar names listed below **indicate** either a common origin, or the **assimilation** by one culture of the traits of another, or lastly that one culture has evolved from another while retaining elements of the mother culture. As I write this, I can think of no other reasonable or rational explanations for the obvious affinity between the Judaic and Babylonian calendars. Of course it would be *naive in the extreme* to think that the associations of the cultures are *limited* to similar calendar terms alone; so, at this time, it behooves us to explore deeper into the practices, lifestyle, and rituals of the ancient Babylonians pursuant to more enlightenment as regards other possible cultural affinities between the Babylonians and Jews.

Judaic	Babylonian	Judaic	Babylonian
Nisan	Nissanu	Tishri	Tishritu
Iyar, Ayar	Aru	Heshvan	Arahsamna
Sivan	Simanu	Kislev	Kislimu
Tammuz	Dumuzu	Tevet, Tebet	Tebetu
Av, Ab	Abu	Shevat, Shebat	Sabatu
Elul	Ululu	Adar	Addaru

Section Two

The Secret Origins Of Judaism

Exploring The Menologies Of Sumerian Calendar In Relation To The Jewish Calendar

The menologies of a calendar are the annotations and commentaries attached to various dates of the calendar that remind or notify us that such and such a date is a Government Holiday, or a Religious Holiday, or perhaps a New Moon or the Beginning of a season or what have you. **It's common for various religious organizations to have notations printed with the calendar dates** that notify the members of said organizations of various Religious Holidays, or Gatherings, or Festivals and the like, attached to the date. **Menologies can be found throughout our society** in several categories, be they business, agriculture, entertainment, sports, theater, and on and on whereas specialty calendars have annotations and commentaries attached to certain dates that mark certain events, functions, or announcements.

This system of calendar menologies goes back thousands of years, and was *thoroughly pervasive* amongst the ancient Sumerians (from whom the Semites copied their system). The menologies of the Sumerians covered every day of the year and every facet of life, **to repeat,** *every day in the year and every facet of life* was annotated on the Sumerian calendars. Unlike us, who greet almost every day with an open agenda, **the Sumerians** *lived by a regulated system* whereas the activities of the community, in total, were *completely* prescribed and *regulated* **from day to day.**

The genesis of the Jewish Sabbath is found within *these ancient menologies* **of the Sumerians** - the link is *firm* and *solid*. The Sumerians *started it*, the Babylonians *continued it,* and the Jews *took it* and made it their own. The Sumerians assigned some days as *Unlucky days* and other days as *Lucky days*; some days were propitious but others were not - the calendar told it all.

Section Two

The Secret Origins Of Judaism

The menologies of their calendar were sort of like a *community horoscope or almanac* that guided the Sumerians, *as a community*, through every single day of the year. On some days they were advised *not to travel*, some days *not to build*, some days *not to do business*, some days *not to receive medical care*, on and on through a multitude of prohibitions. **The Sumerian calendar also advised** when days were *lucky* or *propitious* and favored certain activities. **The calendar prohibitions** of the Sumerians carried the force of law, and the public was faced with punishments if they dared to defy the law.

We are all familiar with the concept of Market Days whereas at *appointed times* during the month the farmers bring their goods into the cities and setup Markets for a day or a few days so that the city dwellers can obtain food supplies - **this system was common throughout the ancient world,** and, of course, still prevails in some locales. **Well, the Sumerian society was structured** so that not only Market Days, Festivals, Holy Days, Sacrificial Days, and the like were engraved upon their calendars, **but also virtually every mundane activity** that might be engaged in had an appointed date or dates on the Sumerian calendars.

There can be no doubt that the Jews copied their calendar system from the Semitic Babylonians; nevertheless it is also important to remember that the original prototype calendar was established by the ancient Sumerians. **The Sumerian civilization flourished** in the Mesopotamian area well back into prehistory. **The Sumerians were not Semites,** but otherwise their ethnicity has not been agreed upon by diverse historians. The issue is not important to our unraveling or uncovering of the true origins of the Jewish Shabbat, so we won't explore the various claims as to the origins of the Sumerians. **It is clear** that the Semitic Tribes that overpowered the Sumerians, in particular the Babylonians, were the conduits through which the Jews, being Semites themselves, were indoctrinated into Sumerian culture.

The ancient Sumerian calendar was not limited to notations of the dates of the months - the calendar, it can be said, *functioned as the guidebook* for the *totality* of Sumerian life, be it commerce, religion, ethics, culture,

Section Two

The Secret Origins Of Judaism

sanitation, education or whatever. **The calendar noted all** the months and days of the year along with notations for each days functions.

The Sumerians noted, not only the religious festivals, sacred days and Sabbaths; **but also** days for cleaning, travel days, days for the Construction of Buildings, marketing days, marriage days, contractual days, days for leaving, days for returning, **and on and on and on**. There were, likewise, days noted as unlucky, and other days noted as lucky, as I indicated above.

In Sumerian society there were days of prohibition, on which specified activities could not be done; such as days prohibiting medical care, days prohibiting legal council, days prohibiting riding in conveyances, days prohibiting the eating of certain foods, days prohibiting traversing the streets, days prohibiting the changing of clothing, days prohibiting the taking of oaths, days prohibiting business activities, days prohibiting hunting and/or fishing. There were days for making sacrifices to the deities and days for *not* making sacrifices, days for prayer and days for *not* praying, there were indeed specifications for each day's activities for all the days of the months and year.

An apt description of the calendar is that the menologies of the *Sumerian State Calendar* incorporated an extremely extensive system of *Cultural Directives* that covered religion, commerce, culture, civic life, ethics, work, leisure, and law, and literally every imaginable facet of life. **I think that it is easily deducible that this Sumerian calendar was a model** by which the Hebrews, in later years, fashioned their own *cultural calendar*, with the absurd claim that their *annual calendar of religious events* was decreed especially for them by god almighty.

Anciently, over the years of Semitic domination of the Sumerians, the Sumerian alphabet and calendar were assimilated by the Aramaeans, Amorites, Assyrians, Babylonians, and other Semitic tribes; later this same Sumerian calendar became source material for the Judaic calendar of the Habiru (Habiri, Hebrews) by way of the Babylonians - this fact cannot be rationally doubted, based on our viewing of the pertinent data.

Section Two

The Secret Origins Of Judaism

We need to keep in mind that the goal of this book, as well as my other astro-theological books, is to decode, or link our modern religious traditions and mythological tales with their *pre-religious origins*; and/or, in some cases, to unveil the underlying encrypted meanings of the rituals and myths embodied within modern religion with interpretations that break through the overlapping spurious, religious veneers; thereby revealing the *core truths* encased or entrapped within the encrypted codes of religious mythology. So before we commence making definitive connections between the Jewish Shabbat and the Sumerian-Babylonian Shabattu, I think that we should first take a wider view of the *initial contacts* of the Semites with the Sumerians in the lands of Mesopotamia, and the *Shabbat origins* as found amongst the ancient Sumerians - going far, far back into time.

According to historians, the Semitic tribes invaded the lands of the ancient Sumerians in two waves, extending over several centuries. The first wave of Semitic tribes came from *southern* Arabia some time before 3000 B.C., and successfully overpowered the Sumerians, thereby eventually establishing the kingdoms of Akkad and Sumer, with the Semites positioned as the Dominant force. As the centuries passed, a second series of Semitic invasions came forth from the regions *west* of Mesopotamia, from a area roughly comparable to modern-day Syria and Lebanon - these invasions took place around 2300 B.C., according to some historians. The result was that, over the centuries, the entire region of Mesopotamia, comparable to modern-day Iraq came under the control of the Semites.

The latter Semitic invaders overpowered Akkad-Sumer, and subsequently founded the Assyrian and Babylonian empires that extended well out beyond the cradle of Mesopotamia into the broader regions of the Middle East or Western Asia. These Semitic invaders, at the time of their initial invasions, were an unlettered people; they did not possess a written language nor a sophisticated culture. The Sumerians, on the other hand, possessed an advanced culture, were highly literate, with an alphabet and calendar. Eventually, the Sumerians were dispersed or erased as a distinct people, and what was once the *Sumerian* language and culture was reborn, in due course and modified form, within a *Semitic* guise. As before stated,

Section Two

The Secret Origins Of Judaism

the brutish Semites assimilated the highly advanced Sumerian culture, adapted it to their likings, and made it their own.

The Semites adopted the calendar of the Sumerians, and along with the calendar came everything else of the ancient Sumerian culture; in that the Sumerian calendar, as we have noted above, covered and directed every facet of Sumerian life. The Semites conquered the Sumerians, marginalized them, and adopted the Sumerian culture, thereby, over time blending the Semitic and Sumerian *cultural* history into one. And going forward from those times of cultural fusion, Sumerian culture and history became, for all practical purposes, *as one* with Semitic culture and history. At that point and time in history, some four to five thousand years ago, the Semites had no history worthy of the name, so they embraced the Sumerian culture and made it their own. The Semites assimilated the Sumerian culture in total, in that, over time, they totally erased or displaced the Sumerian people as an identifiable entity.

Consequently the roots of *Semitic* culture, and the roots of *Judaic* doctrine are clearly and vividly discernable within the historical records of ancient Sumer. Judaic cultural and religious history *begins* with Sumer. And fortunately, this history, that is the Sumer-Semitic history, has been studiously explored by academia and is now available, and indeed, quite readily assessable to our assiduous inquiry and investigation. We are now able to accurately *trace the origins* of the Semitic *deities* and the Jewish *rituals*, in great part, simply by examination of the cultures of old that were most influential on Jewish or Semitic culture, which leads directly to ancient Sumer as the primary source of ancient Semitic traditions.

The Sabbath And The 7-Day Week

Within the last two hundred years or so, the origins of the Jewish people and Judaism has been thoroughly investigated by various Assyriologists from a broad spectrum of academics and scholars of the major European nations, including Germany, France, England, and others. I have assembled my *data*, as presented in portions of the following, from the reviewing of *books* and

The Secret Origins Of Judaism

printed lectures of various of these scholars - highly recommended from the many are Stephen Langdon, Hutton Webster, Theodor Gaster, and Hayyim Schauss.

To begin: The name of the Sumerian *Sabbath* or *Sabbath Equivalent* was "Uhulgallu" which was defined by the Sumerians as "the day when it is dangerous to break the rules". The Babylonians, succeeding the Sumerians, incorporated the term *Sabattu* for Uhulgallu - *Sabattu* means to cease, come to rest, pause, completion or culmination.

The number of Sabbath days utilized by the Sumerians and Semites varied or was subject to tinkering throughout the history of the calendar, as with any of the world's calendars. Of course each and every day in their calendar carried a menology of the do's and don'ts attached to the said date or day, as we have indicated above. The number of days that were *particularly designated as Sabbath* days observed within a given month were eventually reduced from *nine* to *five* Sabbaths. The reduction was made because of the fact that they, like other cultures worldwide, reformed their calendars from time to time, for reasons religious, political, calendrical, economic, or civil.

According to the scholars, initially the Mesopotamians observed *nine* Sabbaths in each month - the Sabbaths occurred on days 1,7,9,14,19,21,28,29, and 30. Day 1 was a Sabbath by reason of the *New Moon*. Days 7,14,21, and 28 were Sabbaths by reason of dividing the light phase of the moon into 4 divisions of 7 days each, spanning from 1-7, 7-14, 14-21, and 21-28. Day 9 has not, to the best of my knowledge, been deciphered by the scholars. Day 19 was designated as *Day of Wrath* in reverence or in reverential fear of the goddess Gula (Bau). The scholars have offered interesting speculations as to why this designation as a *Day of Wrath* was made for Day 19, but we need not explore those *speculations* here at this time. Days 29 and 30 were Sabbaths by reason of the two days of darkness when the moon (Moon god) was not visible or in peril.

The utilization of nine Sabbaths by the Sumerians-Semites came early in the history of their calendar. Subsequently, over the centuries, as the Semites ruled in Mesopotamia, they, the Semites, initiated their own adjustments to

Section Two

The Secret Origins Of Judaism

the calendar. The movement and influences that resulted in a shift from *months containing nine Sabbaths* to *months containing five Sabbaths* stretched over four hundred years; from about 1000 B.C. to 600 B.C. when the transition was completed. **This is important,** because we are now honing in on the final transitions that led to the modern system of *7-day weeks*; that is to say, *the true origins* of the month which has four divisions that number *seven days* each and *four Sabbaths as dividers* of the *weeks* of the month; apart from the ridiculous tale proffered to us by the Hebrews that the Sabbath resulted from their god taking a *break* on the seventh day so as to rest from his labors.

The shift in the calendar from *Nine Rest Days to the month* to *Five Rest Days to the month* was finalized or, perhaps I should say, proclaimed by the notable Assyrian sovereign, King Asurbanipal (Ashurbanipal) in the 7th Century B.C.. Asurbanipal commanded that the *Rest Days* of the calendar be reduced to Days 7, 14, 19, 21, and 28 - the other *Rest Days* were forever eliminated. However, by 600 B.C., according to the scholars, Day 19, as a Sabbath day, had faded from use, leaving only The 7th, 14th, 21st, and 28th days as Sabbath days of the month. The Assyriologists have garnered this information by *actual readings of the records* or documents of the ancient Sumerians-Semites; so *we know* that we are on solid grown with this information.

The system incorporated by the *Assyrians* and *Babylonians* for *numbering the days of each month* was as follows: each month started Day 1 with the *sighting* of the New Moon - from that point on, the 7th, 14th, 21st, and 28th days were counted as *Rest Days* i.e. **Shabbat** days or **Shabattu** days, on which the normal mandatory prohibitions were enforced as we noted earlier in our essay. **Under this system**, the last week of the calendar always carried an odd number of days, because they would not count Day 1 of the next month until the moon arose refreshed, from outer darkness, as the sliver of light that we call the New Moon or *birth* of the New Moon; in other words, the 29th and 30th days, that is to say the 2 or 2 1/2 *moonless* days of the lunar month, were *not* noted in the calendar.

Section Two

The Secret Origins Of Judaism

At some point in between 600 B.C. and 400 B.C., the Habiru, or Hebrews as they are now popularly known, at a time when they were coming into their own as a vibrant, functioning, distinct tribal community, commenced tinkering with the old Semitic calendar of Asurbanipal; and modified it to their own likings. They maintained the 7-day divisions of the month, but they unlocked the Sabbaths (Shabattu) from the 7th, 14th, 21st, and 28th days of the month. **The Jews commenced** counting *all* 29 or 30 days of the lunar month thereby allowing or causing the Sabbath *dates* to occur freely within a given month. Of course the Sabbath (Shabbat) was always the 7th interval between the weekly divisions of the month, but it, the Jewish Sabbath, was now not tied down to any certain dates as with the Babylonian calendar.

The Shabbat (Sabbath) performs the practical function of dividing the lunar month into four whole sections comprised of seven days each. History shows that cultures have tried sectioning the moon cycle with divisors other than the seven, but the *seven* has won out as the most workable number. Worldwide, *seven* was not the only divisor attempted; *two* has been tried, that is, sectioning the moon by its waxing and waning phases, from 1 to 15, and 15 to 30 days; *five* has also been utilized, with six weeks of five days each; *ten* was tried by the Greeks and perhaps others, with three weeks of ten days each, and there have been more variations, but the number 7, over the years, has won the most political acceptance.

Religiously, the Sabbath day was a *taboo* day among the ancient Sumerians, with many deadly prohibitions and superstitions that go far back into pre-history. The Shabbat of the Jews originated as the **Sumerian Uhulgallu**, that is, *"the day when it is dangerous to break the rules"*. The primitive superstitions and rituals of the ancient Sumerians have clearly carried over into the Judaic Sabbath.

As noted above, there were originally nine major Sabbath days amongst the Sumerians in a calendar in which every day of the month was classified as either lucky or unlucky, or had some type of prohibition or stipulation attached to it. Be that as it may, the Sabbaths were exalted above all other

Section Two

The Secret Origins Of Judaism

days of the month, and violation of the Sabbath was punishable by death - and this exact same punishment of death has been biblically applied to the Jewish Sabbath. It is absolutely impossible to rationalize the bible's directive that violators of the Sabbath must be killed; but, at the least, we now know from whence the Jews derived this heinous concept or tradition.

In this brief synopsis of the *Sabbath and the 7-Day Week*, we have tracked the evolution of the Sabbath phenomena amongst the Jews, from its seminal beginnings as *nine Sabbath days* assigned to the month by the ancient Sumerians, some five thousand years ago, to the inception of the *seventh day Sabbath* amongst the Semites some twenty-five hundred years ago. As we can see from the evidence that we have presented, the evolution of the *7-day week* resulted from a series of historical events over several years - and the institution itself, that is the *Sabbath and 7-day Week*, is completely devoid of any godly input.

As Regards Hebrew History Verses Hebrew Myth

It must be again noted that the biblical miracles of the Hebrews do not reflect actual verifiable historical events. The *miraculous* biblical sagas were all *concocted* by the Jewish Rabbis and Sages; the tales are mythological with significant esoteric content, but the history of the Hebrews *as narrated in the bible* is not truthful nor is it legendary. - by *not legendary*, I mean that the bible renditions are not hyped up versions of events that actually took place in history. For instance, some people choose to believe that the tale of the miraculous crossing of the Red Sea by the Hebrews is a wild exaggeration of a true historical event - not so, such events never took place to any degree, but rather reflect pure symbolism.

The Hebrews or Jews become identifiable in secular history, as distinguished from mythology, in the centuries leading up to the Common Era. In order to find a reasonably trustworthy account of the Hebrews prior to (and after) the so-called exile of B.C. 586, we best seek references under the term *Habiru*. There are accounts of the Habiri (Hebrews) in the *Middle*

Section Two

The Secret Origins Of Judaism

East region of ancient times, and unfortunately, all accounts and descriptions of the Habiru (Habiri) i.e. Hebrews are very unflattering.

Again, the Hebrews have published a fabricated, artificial history by means of the Torah and other mythical stories and folklore. It's very difficult for the average lay person to locate authentic secular history as pertaining to the Jews (Hebrews) of old; however the use of the term Habiru, in conjunction with or instead of the term Hebrew, will aid significantly in the search for a reasonably authentic or coherent accounting of that nomadic, wandering people of ancient times that are now popularly labeled as Hebrews; keepers of the Judaic doctrine, a doctrine that when taken literally is blatantly absurd, however *when decrypted* or dislodged from its mythological trappings is supremely venerable - most precious.

The Hebrews, *as described in the bible*, are not findable in non-religious history, only in the bible and Quran. Secular history does not confirm the existent of a great Judaic or Israeli Kingdom. The Habiru, the name from which Hebrew is evidently derived are, indeed, historical. **The Habiru are mentioned in ancient documents** and letters by personalities and officials of the Levant and Middle East; **they are universally described** as bandits, outcasts, mercenaries, raiders, nomadic marauders, migrant workers, and such.

The Hebrews of the bible are totally unknown to Secular History, by that I mean that the Hebrew biblical mythology put forth as actual history is not secularly verifiable. The Habiru (Hebrews) are reasonably well known, and unfortunately carry a notorious reputation, that is, according to the historians that have researched their history. The *biblical Hebrews* cannot be located in secular ancient history *in any way that significantly conforms* with the scriptural narrations of their *alleged* biblical history.

Death For Violation Of The Sabbath

The bible is very forceful in its edict that death is the punishment for violating the Sabbath. The injunction is repeated several times within the bible........*Exodus 31:14 Ye shall keep the sabbath therefore; for it is holy unto you:*

Section Two

The Secret Origins Of Judaism

every one that defileth it shall surely be put to death...... **This same edict is found within the menologies or doctrines of the ancient Sumerians,** in particular *the punishment of death* is instructed for anyone that travels during the dark phase of the moon, that is the 29th and 30th days of the lunar month. Langdon makes reference to this on page 84 of his book *Babylonian Menologies and the Semitic Calendars.* Of course, a major prohibition of the Jewish Sabbath is that the Jews must not travel on the lord's day - this tradition is clearly linked to the ancient reverence and worship of the Moon god, *Sin.* The ancient Semites gave reverence to the sun and the moon, but the Moon god, or, we might say, the god represented by the dynamics of the moon, was their primary deity.

Going back to primordial times, the first traditional Sabbaths observed (Sabbath being defined functionally as lunar periods of *pause, cessation,* or *culmination*) were the *Full Moon* and the *New Moon.* The Full Moon had approximately three days of pause, between the 14th and 17th, as the moon reached fullness and then, after three days, began to wane; and, at the opposite, the approximately three days of darkness, between the 28th and lunar rebirth on the 1st day of the New Moon.

When the moon phased into the darkness of the 29th and 30th days of the month, it was said by the ancient Semites (Assyrians, Babylonians, et al) that the moon (the cosmic image of the moon god, Sin) entered **Irkalla** (a mythological type of Hades, Hell) i.e. the netherworld, the abode or domain of the dead, the realm of **Nergal** - that the moon had crossed over or into the *River of Death,* into the perils of Satan's or Nergal's Domain.

This mythological journey of the moon through the perils of death when it enters its dark phase, and then rebirth as the New Moon is in exact *correspondence* or *parallel* to the solar mythology of the sun also entering into the grave of the Winter Solstice, where it lingered likewise for three days before its rebirth on December 25. So the death and rebirth of the moon was revered anciently just as the death and rebirth of the sun - in fact the scholars place the lunar myth as developing before the solar myth.

Section Two

The Secret Origins Of Judaism

So we can see vividly in the Semitic mythology, that the moon was seen as in the bounds of death, or threatened death during its dark phase, and correspondingly, the ancients instructed, in keeping with their primitive and superstitious mind-set, that anyone that traveled beyond the gate of their residence, during the time of the moon's struggles or sojourn through the river of death, that such person or persons would be subject to the penalty of death. **It was declared**, that during the term of the Moon god's struggle within the cosmic waters of death, **it was incumbent that all mundane activity** *cease* **and** *desist* as they awaited the outcome of the Moon's plight. **And whosoever dared to violate** the sanctity of the moment would, of a certainty, be killed. This, indeed, was the primitive mind of Man in action.

In those early primordial times when the myths first germinated and expanded in Man's unlettered imagination, Man was clueless as to *why* the moon went into darkness, or the sun became enfeebled and obscured, thereby releasing the torrents of winter and darkness upon his soul.

Man's imagination went wild, and his *primitive logic*, which to that point in time, had not been refined by scientific knowledge accompanied by a rational understanding of the real forces of nature, tended to conjure up rituals and ceremonies that seem to defy sanity; that is, from our perspective so many thousands of years later.

I am not puzzled by the *illogical logic* of primitive Man of the long passed primordial eras, nor of the fact that the early civilizations that followed, like those of the Semites, held on to those inherited vacuous concepts and traditions from the distant past. **But I am puzzled** by this: that here in the 21st century there are many folks that ardently declare their belief in these bizarre traditions; and, to this day, adhere with such unrelenting fervor to these inane rituals. Devout Jews adamantly refuse to ride in a conveyance, or light a fire to warm their bodies, or seek medical care on a Sabbath day. They firmly believe that these activities and more are divinely prohibited by god almighty on this special day, called the Sabbath.

As stated repeatedly in my writings, each of our religious myths, traditions, and rituals have evolved from a *pre-religious core*, that was in some way

Section Two

The Secret Origins Of Judaism

connected with Man's interplay with his environment and/or Man's efforts, though at times groping and misguided, to coherently conceptualize the forces that manipulated his environment. Whether dealing with Environmental Mythology or Scientific Mythology[19], the core value is found in our maxim, as expressed and explained in my earlier books on this subject; *Spirits based on Physics* is the theme to remember.

It's important to remember that all of the major feasts, the New Moons, and the Sabbaths are accorded the same reverence and standing in the bible. All of the Seven Jewish Feasts are Sabbaths because they, in fact, function as Sabbaths - with the same and/or similar prohibitions and stipulations as the *Saturday* Sabbaths.

We have before, within this book, traced all of the seven feasts back to their *pre-religious* origins or connections. It remains for us to point out one or two *Semitic links* of the Jewish feasts that are *pre-Judaic*. This is important because that which the monotheists have adopted as a culture that they believe is godly ordained is, in fact, simply the lineage of *Semitic culture* wrapped up in a artificial religious shroud.

The Jewish, Muslim, and Christian biblical and Quranic scriptures are *not* authentic advocates of godly traditions. These books are advocates of *Semitic* traditions. The scriptural commandments of the Bible and Quran are a reflection of *Semitic culture* foisted on the rest of us as godly decrees. The holy days, modes of worship, prayer, dress, rules, laws, and customs practiced by the monotheists all *reflect*, (except for some pagan input through Christmas, Easter, etc), *the customs of the Semites* down through

---

[19] Environmental Mythology identifies the earliest forms of animistic mythology whereas mankind imagined that unseen sprit forces, subject to inducements, controlled the forces of nature, and relayed these impressions through oral traditions and the like. Scientific mythology is defined as the allegorical rendering of encrypted cultural and scientific data by means of mythological tales, signs, and symbols.

Section Two

The Secret Origins Of Judaism

their histories, and have no godly sponsorship whatsoever - the claims of the desert nomads, Jews and Arabs alike, that their way is god's way is a complete fraud.

Cultural Traditions Of The Semitic Peoples

Yom Kippur, the most revered of the Jewish feasts, has clear <u>pre</u>-*Judaic* origins. The Yom Kippur observance, *by whatever name*, was practiced among the Sumerians and subsequently the Semitic tribes long before the Hebrews became Jews, and Judaism became a religion in its own right. The Semites inherited or assimilated the Yom Kippur tradition from the Sumerians.

The Sumerians called the month of Tishri *Dukug*, in their language. **Dukug**, which also has other meanings in reference to the netherworld, was described as the "*month of the holy chamber*" wherein the *fates of mankind were decided and judged*. This mythology applied to the month of *Tishri* and was also mirrored in the month of *Nisan*. Both of these months, which serve as pillars or chambers of the equinoxes, autumnal and vernal, likewise are the *Halls of Judgment* in the mythology.

The span of the equinoctial coordinates, from east to west, divide the upper and lower hemispheres, hence the sun's transits of these coordinates was seen, by the Ancients, as **transitions** between opposing cosmic powers or domains which, *when put in a mythological format*, required *inspection* and *judgment* for those entities that *passed over or descended below* the boundaries between the upper and lower domains. The fact that the Jews call or observe the month of *Tishri* as the month of *Judgment and Atonement* reflects an old, old mythology - mythology engendered by the mind of Man, unaided by godly decree.

The months of Nisan and Tishri mirror each other - this is exemplified in the dates of the festivals of these months, which are in exact correspondence. The 1st, 10th, and 15th of both of these equinoctial months mark special observances amongst the Jews, in reflection of the cosmic balance of these two solar intersections, which, as *twin* coordinates, lie at

Section Two

The Secret Origins Of Judaism

opposite ends of the same cosmic diagonal, which (diagonal) divides the celestial southern and northern hemispheres. In sequence, the *Civil New Year*, the *Day of Atonement*, and *Tabernacles* mark the 1st, 10th, and the 15th of Tishri; and in mirrored reflection, the 1st, 10th, and 15th of the month of Nisan are marked by the *Religious New Year*, the *Selection of the Sacrificial Lamb*, and *Passover*. The *1st* of both months mark the beginning of the year (Civil and Religious), The *10th* of both months are dedicated to god through atonement and/or sacrifices, and the *15th* of both months commence a week long stream of religious ceremonies.

The Passover series of festivals is also found within the annals of ancient Sumerian-Semitic lore. The offering of the First Fruits was traditional among the Semitic Assyrians, and is recorded in their written records of the 10th century B.C. and also anterior to that time, according to Stephen Langdon in his book of 1933, Babylonian Menologies and the Semitic Calendars.

The Assyrian festival of the First Fruits took place under the Full Moon of the first lunar month after the vernal equinox, Nisan, just as with the Hebrews. The Jewish religious feasts are part and parcel of Semitic culture, nothing more. **The Jews have modified the festivals** (Feasts) to their tribal likings, and have painted them with a deceptive religious veneer that suits their societal purposes.

Actually it's customary for advancing societies to *reinterpret* or *reinvent* their cultural traditions as time goes on, so perhaps we shouldn't blame or castigate the Semites for doing what so many others have done; but neither can we look the other way and ignore this religious travesty, in view of the debilitating and misleading effects these sinister theological absurdities have had on the perceptions and beliefs of significant portions of the world's inhabitants.

Judaism is an element of Semitic culture, just as much as Islam and the Arabs - they, the Jews and the Arabs, share the same culture and traditional ways. **The Bible and Quran are the world's chief avenues for disseminating Semitic culture, under a religious guise**. The major

Section Two

The Secret Origins Of Judaism

traditions expounded in the Bible and Quran are identical, because both books were constructed under Semitic influences.

The Jews have adapted culturally to the modern world because of the plasticity and dynamics of *Rabbinic Judaism*; whereas, unfortunately, the Arabs and Muslims in general are locked in a *time warp*, boxed in by cultural and religious precepts of a bygone age that they can't unlatch themselves from; because the Quran represents, to their way of thinking, the *inviolate, unchanging* word of god.

The Jews were smart and visionary - they came up with the *Oral Torah* - the Rabbis claim that they have also the *unwritten word* of god, as well as the Written Word or Torah; and that this *Unwritten Torah* has been passed down secretly from generation to generation within the Sanhedrin or Rabbinic inner circle, so they can, with divine sanction, modify and adapt Judaism, at will, to any eventualities; and simply claim that the change was evoked by god through the Rabbis. **The Arabs and Muslims, however,** *are trapped* theologically in the seventh century, because their book represents itself as the absolute *final word* of god. There is no recognized force within Islam that can negate, modify, or *reinterpret* anything in the Quran; and any modernized *reinterpretations* of the book are sure to be emotionally condemned as religious heresy by the Islamic zealots.

It will take generations for the Islamic hierarchy to correct this problem, in my opinion; as *new born* and more enlightened generations of Islamics emerge with time. This is not only because of the thorough and pervasive *religious* indoctrination of the Islamic masses, but also because doctrinal Islam is as much political as it is religious, if not more so. The political fabric of the vaunted Arab empire of centuries ago was threaded together with Islam, so much so that their empire was often called Mohammedan or Islamic... but I digress.

In line with our subject, focused on the bible as a conduit of Semitic (Jewish and Arab culture), let us explore some verses of the bible alleged as Revelations from god. Many of the verses that we shall analyze and evaluate are actually represented as *god speaking in the first person*, instructing us,

Section Two

The Secret Origins Of Judaism

through the Jews, of his godly will. But when inspected, these verses clearly reveal their overriding *cultural persuasions*, unrelated to any true theological or spiritual edification. **The verses deal with the structures of Semitic culture**, but are relayed to us as divine commands from god in the first person, that is to say, direct from the mouth of god, according to the Bible.

On the subject of marriage amongst the ancient Semites, before the advent of Judaism, Semitic culture was polygamous and male dominated to the extreme. Under Judaism, this culture, for good or for bad, was continued and reinforced, because **under Judaism the Semitic culture became godly ordained** - note the following:

Concubines were a standard among the ancient Semites that could afford them. According to the bible this system is ordained by god: ... *Genesis 25:6 But unto the sons of the concubines, which Abraham had, Abraham gave gifts, and sent them away from Isaac his son, while he yet lived, eastward, unto the east country.......2 Samuel 5:13 And David took him more concubines and wives out of Jerusalem, after he was come from Hebron: and there were yet sons and daughters born to David.*

The Semites did not marry outside of their race or tribe - they would take concubines from among other groups but marriage was restricted to members of their own community....... *Deuteronomy 7:3-4 Neither shalt thou make marriages with them; thy daughter thou shalt not give unto his son, nor his daughter shalt thou take unto thy son. For they will turn away thy son from following me, that they may serve other gods: so will the anger of the LORD be kindled against you, and destroy thee suddenly.*

It was a custom among the pre-Judaic Semites for the men to have children by their slaves (bondmaids) and raise the children within their household, without changing the status of the bondwoman - this is reflected is the bible as pleasing to god.......*Genesis 16:1-3 Now Sarai Abram's wife bare him no children: and she had an handmaid, an Egyptian, whose name was Hagar. And Sarai said unto Abram, Behold now, the LORD hath restrained me from bearing: I pray thee, go in unto my maid; it may be that I may obtain children by her. And Abram hearkened to the voice of Sarai. And Sarai Abram's wife took Hagar her*

Section Two

The Secret Origins Of Judaism

maid the Egyptian, after Abram had dwelt ten years in the land of Canaan, and gave her to her husband Abram to be his wife.......Genesis 30:2-5 And Jacob's anger was kindled against Rachel: and he said, Am I in god's stead, who hath withheld from thee the fruit of the womb? And she said, Behold my maid Bilhah, go in unto her; and she shall bear upon my knees, that I may also have children by her. And she gave him Bilhah her handmaid to wife: and Jacob went in unto her. And Bilhah conceived, and bare Jacob a son.

Also in custom among the Semites, if a brother died without having children by his wife, it was the obligation of a living brother to impregnate his brother's widow so as to bring forth children for his deceased brothers legacy.......Deuteronomy 25:5-6 If brethren dwell together, and one of them die, and have no child, the wife of the dead shall not marry without unto a stranger: her husband's brother shall go in unto her, and take her to him to wife, and perform the duty of an husband's brother unto her. And it shall be, that the firstborn which she beareth shall succeed in the name of his brother which is dead, that his name be not put out of Israel.

As indicated, the ancient Semites were a slave keeping people, but they were discouraged from enslaving fellow Semites - they were taught to seek slaves from foreign races. If ever the Semites enslaved members of their own race/tribe, such slaves were *indentured*, meaning that the individuals bondage was limited to a specified term. **This system was right in keeping with god's directives, according to the bible**.......Leviticus 25:44-46 Both thy bondmen, and thy bondmaids, which thou shalt have, shall be of the heathen that are round about you; of them shall ye <u>buy bondmen and bondmaids.</u> Moreover of the children of the strangers that do sojourn among you, <u>of them shall ye buy, and of their families that are with you,</u> which they begat in your land: and they shall be your possession. And ye shall take them as an inheritance for your children after you, to inherit them for a possession; <u>they shall be your bondmen for ever:</u> but over your brethren the children of Israel, ye shall not rule one over another with rigour.......Exodus 21:2-6 <u>If thou buy an Hebrew servant, six years he shall serve: and in the seventh he shall go out free</u> for nothing. If he came in by himself, he shall go out by himself: if he were married, then his wife shall go out with him. If his master have given him a wife, and she have born him sons or daughters; the wife and her children shall be her master's, and he shall go out by himself. And if the servant shall plainly say, I love my master, my wife, and my children; I will not go

Section Two

The Secret Origins Of Judaism

out free: Then his master shall bring him unto the judges; he shall also bring him to the door, or unto the door post; and his master shall bore his ear through with an aul; and he shall serve him for ever. **So here we have the systems of *direct slavery*** (for foreign races) **and *indentured servitude*** (for members of one's own race), as, for instance, was practiced in early America, **clearly endorsed by the god of the bible.**

God admonished his chosen that they should be good, prudent and just slave holders.......*Exodus 21:20-21 And if a man smite his servant, or his maid, with a rod, and he die under his hand; he shall be surely punished. Notwithstanding, if he continue a day or two, he shall not be punished: for he [i.e. the slave] is his money.*

God commands that criminals be publicly beaten with a whip, but the lashes should be limited to 40 counts.......*Deuteronomy 25:2-3 And it shall be, if the wicked man be worthy to be beaten, that the judge shall cause him to lie down, and to be beaten before his face, according to his fault, by a certain number. Forty stripes he may give him, and not exceed: lest, if he should exceed, and beat him above these with many stripes, then thy brother should seem vile unto thee.*

By god's law, adulterers must be killed; the community shall gather and cast stones against the adulterers till they are dead.......*Deuteronomy 22:23-24 If a damsel that is a virgin be betrothed unto an husband, and a man find her in the city, and lie with her; Then ye shall bring them both out unto the gate of that city, and ye shall stone them with stones that they die; the damsel, because she cried not, being in the city; and the man, because he hath humbled his neighbour's wife: so thou shalt put away evil from among you. Leviticus 20:10 And the man that committeth adultery with another man's wife, even he that committeth adultery with his neighbour's wife, the adulterer and the adulteress shall surely be put to death.*

God advocates public executions, but within limits.......*Deuteronomy 21:22-23 And if a man have committed a sin worthy of death, and he be to be put to death, and thou hang him on a tree: His body shall not remain all night upon the tree, but thou shalt in any wise bury him that day; (for he that is hanged is accursed of god;) that thy land be not defiled, which the LORD thy god giveth thee for an inheritance.*

God says that the rape of a slave woman is less important than the rape of a free woman.......*Deuteronomy 22:25 But if a man find a betrothed damsel in the field, and the man force her, and lie with her: then the man only that lay with her*

The Secret Origins Of Judaism

shall die:...Leviticus 19:20 And whosoever lieth carnally with a woman, that is a bondmaid, betrothed to an husband, and not at all redeemed, nor freedom given her; she shall be scourged; they shall not be put to death, because she was not free.

I have supplied this handful of examples, *out of hundreds within the bible*, to reinforce my assertion that these biblical dictates are clearly and palpably *cultural edicts* derived from ancient *Semitic culture*, and *not* godly commands. **The bible reflects <u>Semitic culture and traditions fraudulently penned under the name of a fictitious Jewish god</u>**. The question that confronts us is this: do these so-called godly directives of the bible reflect the wisdom and justice of god almighty, or is it reasonable to believe that these tenets, in truth, reflect the tenor of the times in which they were written, and are devoid of any divine or godly input.

The stated purpose of this book, from the opening pages, has been to present reasonable and persuasive evidence that the claim of godly patronage by the Jews is completely bogus. In pursuit of this goal of invalidation, we have assailed the Seven Jewish Feasts, touted by the Jews as the nexus of their covenant with god, as actually holdovers from a primitive heathen past. We have presented, I believe, persuasive evidences as to the true origins for the Jewish feasts, and we have rendered explanations of the rituals of the feasts which trace back to their primitive and/or artificial inceptions.

Section Two

The Secret Origins Of Judaism

Epilogue

The bible, in great part, is a book of symbolisms. The bible also reflects, as we have repeatedly indicated within this essay, the culture, attitudes, laws and customs of the ancient Semites. **The Jews have alleged** within their scriptures that the *Law* or the *Torah*, that is to say the book (Torah) that serves as the *guiding force* of Judaic society, was bequeathed especially to the Jewish nation by god almighty himself - this assertion is, of course, pure fantasy. **Be that as it may**, the Jewish Scriptures represent an indispensable treasure trove of the lost wisdom of the Ancients shielded in myths and fables. The fact that the literal renditions of Jewish Lore are palpable nonsense does not, in any way, negate the preciousness of the underlying, encrypted intellectual content of the scriptures. Indeed, the *Wisdom and Secrets of the Ages* have been preserved and secured within this *matrix* called Judaism.

We must preserve this ancient Gnosis at all cost, and actually, I have no doubt that the vital essences of **Esoteric Judaism** will triumph into the indefinite future, under whatever aegis that destiny may appoint. In order for a *pattern of knowledge* to be preserved and carried forward in spirit, throughout the coming eras, **it must have a Host**, a culture in whom the Spirit or Gnosis has embedded itself in a specified expansive form. The Jews have done an excellent job in preserving the Gnosis, but there are indications that the ethnicity of those that call themselves Jews has changed considerably over the eras. This evolution of type will continue into the coming eras in my opinion, so that in the Aquarian Age, **a new** *School* is destined to supplant those of this era, according to what I have learned from others along the way.

The composition of this exposition has not been a frivolous undertaking, nor an academic enterprise pursuant to scoring intellectual points. We are motivated, indeed driven, by a desire to share and to inform - as noted under the type of Jesus in the bible: *of what good is a lighted candle if it is buried*

The Secret Origins Of Judaism

under a bushel.......Matthew 5:15 Neither do men light a candle, and put it under a bushel, but on a candlestick; and it giveth light unto all that are in the house.

We have, as I see it, a *responsibility* to inform others, at least to some degree, when invited or allowed; but *not the right* to *coerce*, or *impose* our opinions on others when our presence is justifiably objected to. **The path** to true Enlightenment and **the attainment** of Enlightenment itself, if it is to be had, must be acquired by the sincere and studious aspirant who is *actively searching* for that *missing something* that his or her soul desires to attach itself to. Again, as noted under the type of Jesus in the bible, we should not seek to impose our views where they are unwelcomed and/or unappreciated; *Matthew 7:6 Give not that which is holy unto the dogs, neither cast ye your pearls before swine, lest they trample them under their feet, and turn again and rend you.*

The parable put forth under the type of Jesus is rather direct and potent; please note however that I do not view people that disagree with me as dogs and swine, as biblically indicated by the referenced verse. **Nevertheless**, the import of the biblical scripture is clear - seeking to impose our views upon others, regardless of how strongly we may perceive the correctness of our views, or attempting to persuade others against their will, inevitably causes stress, opposition and emotional friction, and seldom resolves anything. **When it comes to religion**, people are very territorial - they are not objective and dispassionate, or even reasonable when they feel that their personal beliefs are being attacked. **The immediate response** of the average believer is to *impulsively* defend their traditional beliefs, often irrationally and illogically, but such is the conditioned and/or instinctive response of most people when they feel that their *space* has been invaded.

We do not need the agreement of others to affirm the correctness of our research - **the facts speak** *loudly* for themselves. **I recognize and support** the rights of others to follow the cultural and religious paths of their choosing. **However**, any religion that advocates itself before the public domain, and seeks the recognition and respect of the public and governments as regards its customs, rituals, doctrines, holy days, and desires, should, I believe, be subject to our public critiques. Considering the

Epilogue

The Secret Origins Of Judaism

momentous impact of Judaism on the ancient and modern worlds; directly, and through its offshoots Christianity and Islam, the *Jewish exoteric doctrine, I think, should be subjected to the highest most strenuous Public scrutiny* that the world can muster - pursuant to an elevated state of awareness and understanding for us all in the aftermath of our investigation.

We have done our best within this essay, to help recommence a vigorous examination and, indeed, investigation of the spurious, and absurd *religious* and *political* assertions of the Jews. **According to the bible**, the Jews are the *son of god*, and also, **according to the bible**, the Jews are appointed by god to rule this world. .... *Exodus 4:22 And thou shalt say unto Pharaoh, Thus saith the LORD, Israel is my son, even my firstborn:* .... **Deuteronomy 7:6** *For thou [Israel] art an holy people unto the LORD thy God: the LORD thy God hath chosen thee to be a special people unto himself, above all people that are upon the face of the earth.*

Epilogue

The Secret Origins Of Judaism

Index

A

Abraham, 15, 119, 129, 148
Adam, 57, 118
Allegory, 64, 69, 73, 144
Altar, 58, 104, 106, 107, 108
Amorites, 134
Ancient, 19
Arabs, 8, 23, 128, 145, 146, 147
Aramaeans, 134
Aries, 53
Ark, 55, 99, 103
Assyrians, 134, 135, 138, 142, 146
Astrological, 19, 57, 58, 86, 101, 125
Astronomical, 55
Astronomy, 21
Atonement, 5, 7, 8, 13, 14, 16, 17, 23, 61, 62, 81, 82, 87, 94, 96, 98, 100, 102, 104, 105, 106, 107, 108, 111, 127, 145, 146
Autumnal, 13, 18, 59, 60, 62, 64, 80, 81, 82, 85, 86, 96, 110, 145
Autumnal Equinox, 13, 18, 59, 60, 62, 64, 81, 82, 85, 86, 110

B

Babylon, 78, 127, 128, 129, 130, 131, 135, 139, 142, 146

Bear, 59, 77, 107, 149
Bikkurim, 5, 12, 26, 66, 67, 70, 75, 76, 80
Book Of Life, 101

C

Calendar, 80, 81, 83, 84, 85, 86, 87, 88, 89, 90, 91, 92, 93, 95, 96, 97, 98, 125, 126, 127, 128, 131, 132, 133, 134, 135, 136, 137, 138, 139
Cardinal Point, 18, 19, 41, 64, 86, 110
Cave, 8
Celestial, 19, 55, 97, 146
Chamber, 145
Christianity, 4, 9, 11, 12, 24, 27, 57, 61, 62, 72, 73, 74, 75, 118, 120, 144, 154
Cloven, 27, 73
Conception, 121
Conjunction, 141
Constellation, 93, 128
Core, 23, 24, 33, 34, 35, 36, 46, 53, 56, 63, 68, 117, 128, 135, 143
Cosmic, 5, 51, 53, 55, 57, 59, 60, 61, 80, 82, 84, 87, 91, 94, 110, 125, 128, 142, 143, 145
Cosmos, 54, 88

The Secret Origins Of Judaism

Creation, 124
Cross, 42, 62, 113
Culture, 119
Cycle, 21, 58, 59, 84, 85, 86, 87, 88, 89, 90, 92, 93, 96, 97, 98, 103, 111, 125, 126, 139

D

Darkness, 17, 46, 51, 82, 85, 86, 91, 114, 137, 138, 142, 143
David, 8, 78, 103, 109, 148
Deity, 71, 102
Devil, 17, 63

E

Easter, 23, 62, 144
Eden, 16, 57
Egg, 31, 50, 51, 53
Environmental Mythology, 19, 21, 34, 54, 69, 144
Esoteric, 4, 6, 69, 140, 152
Eve, 57
Evolution, 16, 18, 19, 22, 67, 69, 93, 112, 122, 140, 152
Exoteric, 154

F

Feast, 102
Feasts, 4, 5, 6, 7, 12, 13, 14, 15, 18, 19, 21, 25, 26, 27, 29, 32, 40, 41, 42, 44, 46, 47, 66, 67, 68, 70, 72, 73, 74, 75, 76, 79, 80, 81, 91, 92, 94, 101, 102, 103, 104, 109, 110, 113, 115, 117, 118, 122, 124, 125, 126, 129, 144, 145, 146, 151
Festival, 102
Fire, 101, 102
Forty Days, 56, 60, 61, 62, 63, 64, 65, 110
Full Moon, 113, 126, 142, 146

G

Garden, 16, 57
Gentile, 12, 110
Gnosis, 152
Goat, 25, 28, 38, 105, 106, 107
Gregorian, 125

H

Habiru, 134, 139, 140, 141
Hades, 142
Hag Hamatzah, 5, 12, 29, 44, 80
Haroseth, 31, 32, 50, 51
harvest, 102
Hebrew, 4, 11, 15, 18, 30, 33, 44, 47, 48, 51, 66, 70, 71, 81, 82, 84, 87, 88, 90, 91, 92, 93, 95, 98, 100, 101, 114, 117, 134, 138, 139, 140, 141, 145, 146
Heliacal, 128
Hell, 142
Hemisphere, 41, 51, 55, 82, 94
History, 119
Horizon, 58, 85

Index

156

The Secret Origins Of Judaism

I

Ioannes, 60
Islam, 4, 9, 11, 12, 23, 75, 118, 146, 147, 154
Israel, 12, 13, 14, 15, 25, 26, 33, 37, 38, 44, 51, 55, 67, 70, 71, 72, 74, 77, 79, 85, 93, 99, 101, 102, 104, 105, 106, 107, 108, 115, 122, 123, 149, 154
Israelite, 15, 18, 25, 26, 27, 29, 30, 31, 55, 68, 70, 71, 73, 78, 79, 102, 115, 141

J

Jacob, 15, 79, 149
Jerusalem, 78, 90, 99, 103, 104, 109, 113, 115, 118, 148
Jesus Christ, 7, 8, 19, 23, 55, 56, 57, 58, 59, 61, 63, 72, 86, 101, 125
Jew, 101, 102
Jewish, 101, 102
John, 56, 57, 58, 59, 60, 61
Judaism, 1, 4, 5, 9, 11, 12, 15, 16, 18, 33, 34, 35, 36, 40, 42, 43, 47, 52, 66, 75, 77, 78, 83, 91, 101, 103, 109, 110, 112, 117, 118, 120, 123, 130, 136, 145, 146, 147, 148, 152, 154
Judgment, 101, 102

Judgment, Judge, 5, 8, 20, 57, 68, 86, 87, 92, 93, 94, 98, 101, 145, 150

K

King, 78, 97, 103, 109, 138

L

Lamb, 14, 25, 26, 28, 29, 30, 31, 41, 42, 50, 53, 96, 146
Leap year, 84, 96, 98
Leap Year, 85, 89, 98, 125
Leaven, 5, 26, 28, 29, 42, 43, 44, 45, 46, 47, 48, 52, 53, 70, 75
Longitude, 91
Lunar, 80, 84, 85, 86, 87, 88, 89, 92, 93, 95, 96, 97, 98, 125, 126, 128, 138, 139, 142, 146
Lunar Month, 84, 89, 96, 97, 138, 139, 142, 146
Lunar Year, 88, 95

M

Mary, 8
Mesopotamia, 18, 128, 129, 130, 133, 135, 137
Metonic, 84, 88, 89, 90, 92, 96, 125
Moon, 17, 58, 76, 83, 84, 86, 88, 89, 90, 91, 93, 125, 126, 137, 138, 139, 142, 143

Index

The Secret Origins Of Judaism

Moses, 7, 13, 14, 15, 26, 27, 37, 71, 72, 73, 74, 77, 79, 80, 99, 101, 102, 105, 108, 115, 122, 123
Mother, 8, 88, 131
Myth, 19, 30, 57, 58, 64, 86, 101, 102, 109, 119, 125, 140, 142
Mythical, 19, 24, 64, 72, 73, 109, 141
Mythological, 119
Mythology, 5, 6, 19, 20, 21, 53, 54, 55, 57, 58, 60, 64, 68, 69, 81, 128, 135, 140, 141, 142, 143, 144, 145

N

Nature, 8, 16, 17, 18, 19, 20, 24, 34, 54, 56, 66, 81, 88, 90, 111, 112, 118, 143, 144
New Moon, 25, 83, 84, 86, 88, 89, 90, 91, 94, 96, 104, 126, 132, 137, 138, 142, 144
New Year, 13, 14, 62, 80, 82, 85, 87, 93, 95, 101, 102, 114, 116, 146
Nisan, 12, 13, 25, 28, 42, 55, 82, 85, 94, 96, 101, 131, 145, 146
nomadic, 19

P

Parallel, 8, 53, 54, 55, 70, 71, 72, 74, 85, 86, 125, 142

Passover, 5, 12, 13, 24, 25, 26, 28, 29, 30, 31, 33, 35, 36, 37, 40, 41, 42, 43, 45, 46, 47, 49, 51, 52, 53, 55, 56, 61, 64, 66, 70, 71, 73, 76, 80, 81, 94, 96, 113, 146
Pesach, 5, 12, 80, 81, 113
Pharaoh, 25, 32, 71, 154
Phase, 21, 58, 60, 75, 137, 142, 143
Physics, 144
Pillar, 12, 18, 23, 145
Pisces, 24
Polar, 57
Priest, 12, 37, 77, 99, 103, 105, 106, 107
Priesthood, 4, 7, 18, 24, 34, 36, 40, 41, 42, 45, 47, 52, 63, 67, 69, 77, 80
Primal, 4, 8, 33, 34, 35, 36, 63, 108
Primitives, 4, 5, 8, 16, 17, 18, 20, 24, 27, 33, 34, 35, 36, 37, 41, 45, 46, 52, 54, 55, 56, 62, 63, 65, 66, 67, 75, 77, 100, 108, 109, 110, 111, 112, 118, 120, 126, 129, 139, 143, 151
Primordial, 5, 8, 16, 17, 19, 20, 21, 24, 33, 35, 36, 41, 47, 48, 53, 56, 63, 64, 111, 142, 143

Index

The Secret Origins Of Judaism

Q

Quran, 4, 7, 8, 15, 30, 118, 141, 144, 146, 147

R

Rabbis, 26, 29, 30, 36, 42, 43, 51, 63, 68, 71, 77, 78, 85, 88, 92, 93, 96, 100, 103, 109, 118, 140, 147
Ram, 102
Religion, 19, 24
Religious, 119
Resurrection, 55, 57, 73
Revelations, 147
rituals, *24*
Rituals, 24
Rosh Hashanah, 5, 13, 14, 62, 80, 82, 85, 86, 87, 93, 94, 95, 98, 101, 102, 110

S

Sabbath, 5, 6, 13, 14, 27, 67, 70, 72, 73, 75, 85, 89, 91, 93, 96, 98, 100, 101, 108, 111, 115, 122, 123, 124, 125, 126, 127, 129, 132, 136, 137, 138, 139, 140, 141, 142, 143
Sacerdotal, 18, 37
Sacrifice, 7, 8, 23, 33, 41, 42, 104, 105
Satan, 11, 56, 60, 61, 63, 142

Saturday, 70, 72, 73, 93, 122, 124, 126, 127, 144
Savior, 56, 57, 115
Scapegoat, 57, 105, 107
Scientific, 4, 5, 6, 19, 21, 34, 54, 69, 143, 144
Seder, 5, 30, 31, 32, 49, 50, 51, 52, 53, 64
Semites, 1, 7, 8, 15, 16, 18, 22, 24, 33, 34, 36, 37, 40, 41, 43, 45, 46, 47, 48, 53, 54, 65, 66, 67, 69, 71, 81, 86, 96, 104, 108, 117, 118, 127, 128, 129, 130, 132, 133, 134, 135, 136, 137, 138, 139, 140, 142, 143, 144, 145, 146, 147, 148, 149, 151, 152
Shabattu, 127, 135, 138, 139
Shabbat, 124, 125, 126, 127, 129, 133, 135, 138, 139
Shavuot, 5, 13, 27, 68, 70, 72, 73, 74, 75, 76, 79, 80, 81, 113
Sheaf, 13, 14, 26, 67, 70, 72, 73, 75, 76
Shepherd, 41, 81, 121
Sin, 76, 86, 91, 142
Slave, 15, 25, 27, 30, 31, 33, 34, 47, 49, 50, 51, 148, 149, 150
Solar year, 88, 96
Solomon, 78, 103, 104, 109, 113
Sourdough, 44, 46, 47, 52, 53
spirit, 19
Spirit, 19
Spiritual, 19

Index

The Secret Origins Of Judaism

Sukkoth, 5, 13, 81, 82, 94, 95, 101, 102, 110, 113, 114, 115, 116, 117, 118, 127
Sumerian, Sumer, 69, 104, 127, 128, 132, 133, 134, 135, 136, 137, 138, 139, 140, 142, 145, 146
Summer Solstice, 18, 58, 86, 110
Sun God, 17
Sunday, 62, 72, 73

T

Tabernacles, 5, 13, 14, 77, 81, 82, 99, 102, 103, 104, 105, 106, 107, 108, 114, 127, 146
Tammuz, 13, 58, 131
Temple, 26, 58, 67, 68, 70, 71, 72, 73, 75, 76, 77, 78, 99, 103, 104, 105, 109, 113
Theology, 13
Time, 24
Torah, 4, 7, 12, 36, 66, 72, 73, 75, 76, 77, 78, 79, 87, 88, 92, 102, 104, 109, 113, 116, 118, 141, 147, 152
Traditional, 6, 24, 28, 30, 36, 48, 49, 63, 76, 84, 103, 109, 116, 118, 126, 142, 146, 153
Traditions, 119
Tribes, 4, 15, 35, 43, 47, 64, 66, 67, 69, 90, 118, 127, 128, 129, 133, 134, 135, 145, 148, 149
Tropical Year, 41, 87, 89

U

Underworld, 51, 53, 55, 58, 59, 60, 61, 85, 94, 111
Universe, 7, 99, 103, 122, 124
Unleavened, 5, 12, 13, 25, 26, 29, 30, 31, 42, 43, 44, 46, 47, 50, 53, 80, 114

V

Vernal Equinox, 13, 18, 23, 25, 41, 46, 51, 53, 55, 56, 59, 60, 61, 62, 64, 66, 80, 82, 86, 87, 89, 94, 110, 146
Virgin, 7, 150

W

Week, 6, 45, 46, 71, 76, 122, 136, 138, 140, 146
Wilderness, 60, 63, 79, 102, 105, 107, 111, 116, 117, 123
Winter Solstice, 18, 23, 58, 59, 86, 110, 142

Y

Yom Hadin, 102
Yom Kippur, 5, 13, 62, 81, 82, 87, 94, 95, 96, 97, 98, 99, 100, 101, 102, 103, 104, 105, 108, 109, 110, 111, 145